Seminars
Fine Arts

Murphy Almeida

2020

After 5 years, texts on Fine Arts are compiled. The purpose of this book is to make known to the general public some texts on specific topics of Fine Arts.

On the other hand, it will also provide a basis for young Masters students or higher education levels (Advanced Studies), as well as teachers who wish to present these themes in the context of a seminar.

Translated by the author, first edition.

Index

Pre-Academy of Fine Arts

The study of artistic education involves three interconnected aspects:

• The institutions where it takes place - Academies or Workshops;

• Theoretical conception of artistic creation;

• Social situation of the artist.

In the Middle Ages, professions linked to the arts are considered craft arts and taught by masters in their workshops, for a period of 3 to 9 years. In this chronological period, the artist is comparable to any other craftsman and the same term "artist" did not exist in the Renaissance[1].

On the other hand, the knowledge we have is only at the documentary level on the organization of trades. For example, they were aware of how to make pigments, technical data passed down from generations.

The painters are included in one of the mastership corporations of the Flag of São Jorge, along with blacksmiths, swordsmen, coppersmiths, artillery smelters, etc.[2] With statute of royal painters, these were considered in the 16th century as mechanics and only in 1698, with the Accordion with Pedro II did painting and sculpture were considered noble arts[3].

---

[1] CHASTEL, André, 'O Artista' in *O Homem Renascentista*, Lisboa, Presença, 1991, p. 171.

[2] COSTA, Félix, *The antiquity of the art of painting*, New Haven, Yale Universlty, 1967, p. 19.

LOUSÃ, Teresa, *Francisco de Holanda e a Ascensão do Pintor*, Tese de doutoramento, FBAUL, 2001, p. 83.
SERRÃO, Vítor, *O maneirismo e o estatuto social dos pintores portugueses*, Lisboa, Imprensa nacional – Casa da Moeda, 1983, p. 68.

[3] COSTA, *op. cit.*, p. 22.

However, Gregório Lopes, a royal painter, at one point receives the Order of Santiago We then have two systems of work: workshop, the most common; and partnerships, such as the Ferreirim Retable, which brought together important names such as Gregório Lopes, Garcia Fernandes and Cristóvão de Figueiredo[4].

In the 15th and 16th centuries, painters worked in workshops, with masters and disciples and often associated themselves with large productions.

We then have two systems of work: workshop, the most common; and partnerships, such as the Ferreirim Retable, which brought together important names such as Gregório Lopes, Garcia Fernandes and Cristóvão de Figueiredo [5]. These partnerships could also emerge from family ties.

Francisco de Holanda (1517-1585), the first artist and theorist of the Renaissance and Mannerism, writes *Do Tirar pelo Natural*, in 1549, in the form of dialogue, explaining how the portrait takes place[6].

SANTOS, Luís Reis, 'Paineis dos Mestres de Ferreirim de igrejas e conventros de Évora', in *Sep. de A cidade de Évora do Boletim da Câmara Municipal de Évora*, numerous 21 e 22, 1950, pp. 9-28.

CASIMIRO, Luís Alberto, 'Pintura e Escultura do Renascimento no Norte de Portugal', in *Ciências e Técnicas do Património*, Revista da Faculdade de Letras na Universidade do Porto, 2006-2007, I Série, Volume V-VI, pp. 87-114. Available at http://ler.letras.up.pt/uploads/ficheiros/6620.pdf [02-01-2014].

[4] *Cf.* CAETANO, Joaquim Oliveira, 'Gregório Lopes – Pintor Régio e Cavaleiro de Santiago', in *As Ordens Militares em Portugal e no Sul da Europa*, Atas do II Encontro sobre Ordens Militares, Lisboa, Edições Colibri / Câmara Municipal de Palmela, 1997.

[5] SANTOS, Reinaldo dos, *Os primitivos portugueses: 1450-1550*, Lisboa, Academia Nacional de Belas Artes, 1940, pp. 16 e 23.

[6] *Cf.* HOLANDA, Francisco de, *Do tirar pelo natural*, Lisboa, Livros Horizonte, 1984.

In this work, the author tells that he went to Santiago de Compostela and passed through Porto, where he contacted Brás Ferreira, discussing the theory of "portraying" with him. When he returns from Santiago, he separates from the Infante and mentions the existence of plaster and the copies are basic elements of artistic education[7]. Although it does not refer to the way they were used, it does refer to the existence of plaster busts from Rome.

At the Academies, drawing and painting and sculpture practice were taught in workshops. Teaching was based on theoretical and historical monitoring to help with the themes. For Francisco de Holanda, the artist had to have a solid theoretical learning and a total commitment to each of the disciplines.

This theorist is also inspired by Neoplatonic theories that he contacted in Italy, with Miguel Ângelo, affirming that God is the first artist, creator of the world and of man. This affirmation gives the artist the gift of creation and moves him away from the workshop, just as he believes in innate talent and each one develops that stimulus.

The painter's masters are nature and antiquity (proportion, beauty, grace and perfection). Giorgio Vasari in 1550 states that Miguel Ângelo achieves perfection in imitating nature and antiquity[8].

In the work Da Ciência do Desenho, from 1571, Francisco de Holanda states that the painter copies ideas that are in his own style and differentiates "Natural Drawing" and "Internal Drawing"[9]. The latter consists of designing the work before carrying it out. In this theory of art, due to the *à maniera*, the

---

[7] Idem, pp. 11/12.

[8] VASARI, Giorgio, *Le vite de' piú eccellenti pittori, scultori e architettori*, Novara, Istituto Geografico de Agostini, 1967, p. 305.

[99] HOLANDA, Francisco de, *Da Ciência do Desenho*, Lisboa, Livros Horizonte, *fl. 37r* e *fl. 37v.°*.

artist starts from the spirit, contact with God to accomplish the work and stops being manual to be considered liberal artist[10].

With D. Sebastião and because oil painters protested taxes as mechanical officers, they opened inquiries and to enter the São Jorge Flag[11]. As early as 1539, the "law on the insertion of artists" allows them to exercise their arts without obligation and to make their children experts (family character)[12].

In 1602, the Brotherhood of São Lucas was founded in Lisbon, at the Monastery of the Annunciation [13] . This Brotherhood was not an academy, but had as its patron Saint Lucas and with the 1755 earthquake, the Church and Monastery of the Announced disappear[14].

In Florence, the Brotherhood of Saint Luke is also located in a Monastery of the Annunciation and tempera painters, illuminators, sculptors and architects could belong. At this time, Drawing is the father of all arts.

In addition to artistic production, this Brotherhood in Lisbon had social functions and did not develop the design academy as it did in Italy and France in the 16th century.

Filipe Nunes, a reference in Portuguese art theory, emerges at the time of the Philippine rule and will carry out his

---

[10] Idem, Capítulo 1.°, *fl. 34r* e *fl. 34v.*°.

[11] SERRÃO, Vítor, *A Pintura Maneirista em Portugal,* Lisboa, Ministério da Educação, 1992, p. 143.

[12] SERRÃO, *O maneirismo e o estatuto...,* p. 167.

[13] COSTA, (Félix) *op. cit.,* p. 19.

Cf. SERRÃO, Vítor, 'O Pintor Régio Fernão Gomes, O Mosteiro da Anunciada e a Fundação da Irmandade de São Lucas, Corporação dos Pintores de Lisboa, em 1602' in GOMES, Ana Cristina, MOURÃO, José Augusto, FRANCO, José Eduardo & SERRÃO, Vítor (Coord.), *Monjas Dominicanas. Presença, Arte e Património em Lisboa,* Lisboa, Alétheia Editores, 2008, p. 112-121.

SERRÃO, *O maneirismo e o estatuto...,* p. 157.

[14] Idem, p. 163.

work *Art da pintura, symmetria, e perspectiva*[15]. For the first time, a didactic work is carried out, aimed at students and disciples, describing the manufacture of paints as they were used in medieval monasteries[16].

This work aims to improve the quality of the painting and is based on the works of Vitruvius (~ 70-25 B.C.)[17], Albrecht Dürer (1471-1528)[18], Daniele Barbaro (1513-1570)[19] and João de Arfe.

In the case of Architecture, it has the most consolidated teaching since the 16th century with the Paço da Ribeira Risk Class, by Filipe II (1527-1598)[20].

With the Restoration of 1640, the problems of D. João IV (1604-1656) are to defend against Spanish invasion and thus invest in fortified and border works. The golden years for military engineers in Portugal.

In 1647, the Fortifications and Military Architecture Class was created, which will be the basis of excellence in the quality of Portuguese constructions, with emphasis on the names of Luís Serrão Pimentel (1613-1679), Azevedo Fortes (1660-1749) and Manuel da Maia (1677-1768)[21].

---

[15] *Cf.* NUNES, Filipe, *A Arte da pintura, symmetria, e perspectiva*, Porto, Paisagem, 1982.

[16] CALADO, Margarida, 'Desenhar o corpo – uma metodologia de ensino constante na arte ocidental', in *Representações do corpo na ciência e na arte*, Lisboa, 2012, p. 117.

[17] *Cf.* VITRÚVIO, *Tratado de Arquitectura*, Lisboa, Instituto Superior Técnico Press, 2006.

[18] *Cf.* DÜRER, Albrecht, *The Painter's Manual*, Connecticut, Abaris Books, 1977.

[19] *Cf.* BARBARO, Daniel, *La Pratica della perspettiva*, [s.n.], C. et R. Borgominièri fratelli, 1568.

[20] CALADO, Margarida & FERRÃO, Hugo, 'Da Academia à Faculdade de Belas-Artes', in *A Universidade de Lisboa nos séculos XIX-XX*, Lisboa, Universidade de Lisboa, Volume 2, pp. 1108.

[21] Ibidem.

Some years later, in 1689, D. Pedro II (1825-1891) published "Regimento dos Mestres Arquitectos dos Paços Reais", on civil architecture, but linked to royal works such as Mafra and Ajuda (18th and 19th centuries)[22].

The absence of a drawing academy led Félix da Costa, at the end of the 17th century, to write the work *The Antiquity of the Art of Painting*, where he draws the attention of D. Pedro II to the need to create an academy[23].

Félix da Costa establishes a hierarchy of painters, in which he distinguishes regular and scientific practitioners, copyists of other paintings and image painters, upholsters and gilders[24].

Bento Coelho da Silveira (1620-1708) was honored, in 1670, by the Singular Academy and this elite where he belonged and, for being cultured, would represent the preparation of the environment for the creation of an academy where he himself would be the director[25]. However, this never came to fruition.

D. João V (1689-1750) had the political and financial will to protect the arts. However, in order to found an academy, it was necessary to have a suitable teacher, so the alternative was to open the country to foreign artists.

At this time, works are imported and the Academy of Portugal is created in Rome for students to contact the Italian masters. They stayed in student-owned residences and were free to attend the studio of local artists.

---

[22] RIBEIRO, Rúben, 'A Barra da Cidade do Porto. Breves Apontamentos', in *Atas do IX Encontro Nacional de Estudantes de História*, Porto, Faculdade de Letras da Universidade do Porto, Biblioteca digital, 2014, pp. 149-165. Available at http://ler.letras.up.pt/uploads/ficheiros/12130.pdf [02-01-2015].

[23] COSTA, (Félix) *op. cit.*, p. 23.

[24] LOUSÃ, *op. cit.*, p. 189.

[25] SOBRAL, Luís de Moura, *Pintura e Poesia na época barroca*, Lisboa, Editorial Estampa, 1994, pp. 17-48.

Machado de Castro (1731-1822) mentions in his work *Discurso sobre as utilidades do Desenho* that D. João V wanted to establish an Academy in Lisbon to house the plasters that came from Rome[26].

Inácio da Piedade Vasconcelos (1676-1752) will produce *Artefactos symmetriacos, e geometricos*[27], intended for students, written in Portuguese, compiled in 4 books and using as sources: Vitruvius (1st century BC), Albrecht Dürer (1471-1528), Daniele Barbaro (1513-1570), João de Arfe (1535-1595) and Jerónimo Penha de Bologna (unknown)[28]. This work represents the first in Portuguese that systematizes artistic practice, in Portuguese, conducts the study from the bones to the skin. On the other hand, this author also suggests the use of naked figures as a method of learning, as happened in European academies.

In 1752, José Gomes da Cruz (unknown) writes *Carta Apologetica y Analytica, que pela ingenuidade da pintura, em quanto sciencia escreveu...*, at the request of André Gonçalves, whose main complaint is the fact that they are still considered mechanical officers[29]. After the earthquake, Vieira Lusitano and André Gonçalves join forces to form a Nude Academy, but it did not last more than an hour[30].

In the second half of the 18th century, new forms of teaching began to emerge in Lisbon and, in particular, with Passos Manuel (1801-1862) in the speech of the foundation of

---

[26] CALADO, *Desenhar o corpo...*, p. 118.

[27] *Cf.* VASCONCELOS, Inácio da Piedade, *Artefactos symmetriacos, e geometricos*, Lisboa, Joseph Antonio da Sylva, 1733.

[28] CALADO, *Desenhar o corpo...*, p. 119.

[29] *Cf.* CRUZ, José Gomes da, *Carta Apologetica y Analytica, que pela ingenuidade da pintura, em quanto sciencia escreveu...*, Lisboa, Na Regia Offic. Sylviana: Academia Real, 1752.

[30] *Cf.* CALADO, Margarida, 'Ensino', in *Dicionário de Art Barroca*, (Dir.) PEREIRA, José Fernandes, Lisboa, Editorial Presença, 1989, pp. 160-163.

the Convento de Mafra, reflecting that space erected as the most recent sculpture school in Portugal.

In 1766, the Drawing and Civil Architecture Class was created at the Royal College of Nobles[31]. Still in the Pombaline context and two years later, the Printmaking Class is created in Lisbon, with the Imprensa Régia, lasting almost 20 years.

In 1770, Machado de Castro created the Sculpture Class and, two years later, the Drawing and Architecture Class was created at the Faculty of Mathematics at the University of Coimbra.

In 1780, Cyrillo Volkmar Machado created the Academia do Nu, but it will only function for one year[32]. Between this period and until 1802, Public Drawing Classes and the Escola da Ajuda were created, with the objective of working on sculpture to integrate the building of the Palace (Machado de Castro and disciples)[33].

Of these schools created, the most important is that of Machado de Castro, with methodologies of the creative process that began in the design of prints and copies and then yes, modeling in clay and stone[34].

---

[31] VIEIRA, José António Jacinto, *História contemporânea da segurança e saúde na fase de concepção arquitectónica*, Dissertação de Doutoramento, Universidade Portucalense Infante D. Henrique, 2007, p. 17.

[32] CALADO, Margarida, 'Desenhar o corpo – uma metodologia de ensino constante na arte ocidental', in *Representações do corpo na ciência e na arte*, Lisboa, 2012, p. 120.

RIBEIRO, Rogério, *A aula de desenho: Academias dos Séc. XIX e XX das Escolas de Belas Artes*, Almada, Câmara Municipal, 1989, p. 20.

[33] Idem, pp. 21/22.

COSTA, Luiz Xavier, *Ensino das Belas Artes nas obras do Real Palácio da Ajuda (1892-1833)*, Lisboa, Academia Nacional de Belas-Artes, 1936, p. 19.

[34] CASTRO, Machado, *Dicionário de escultura*, Lisboa, Livraria Coelho, 1937, pp. 13-19.

These classes show a theoretical and practical character and are linked to the equestrian statue, the Basilica da Estrela and the Ajuda Palace.

In 1836 the Academy of Fine Arts was founded in Lisbon and Porto. Francisco de Assis Rodrigues (1801-1877), with the foundation of this academy, will continue the method of Machado de Castro.

Exasperated modernity

The theories arising in the inter-war period, Arthur Schopenhauer (1788-1860) stands out, where the interrogation is not based on the object, but on the relationship of this object with the viewer[35].

With Nietzsche, with influences from the previous author, in his work *Origem da tragédia*, he will impose a matrix of the meaning of the tragedy - Dionysian spirit. This matrix of the unconscious is revealed only from the mask of Dionysus[36].

The principle of the individual loses the subject-world separation and it breaks, brilliantly represented in the work Munch's *Scream*: the scream that comes out of the subject and spreads the pain in the cosmos [37].

We then have an Expressionism with a more Apollonian shape and dimension, based on gesture and *deformatio*[38]. This distortion makes them grotesque and represents a projection of the subject himself [39]. The themes are not dramatic, but they denote a dramatic charge through painting - this deformation is a gesture that manifests itself[40].

---

[35] SCHOPENHAUER, Arthur, *El mundo como voluntad y representación*, Mexico, Porrúa, 1897, pp. 20/21.

DIAS, Fernando Rosa, *Ecos expressionistas na pintura portuguesa entre-guerras (1914-1940)*, Lisboa, Campo da Comunicação, 2011, p. 17.

[36] *Cf.* NIETZSCHE, Friedrich, *A origem da tragédia*, Lisboa, Guimarães Editores, 1994.

DIAS, Fernando Rosa, *Ecos expressionistas na pintura portuguesa entro-guerras (1914-1940)*, Lisboa, Campo da Comunicação, 2011, p. 19.

[37] Ibidem.

[38] DIAS, *Ecos expressionistas...*, p. 21.

[39] Idem, p. 148.

[40] Idem, p. 233.

More than the form itself, it is the action behind the form, as for example in Paul Pollock (1912-1956) and the theater of action that is worth more than the work itself.

With Wilhelm Worringer (1881-1965) we have a more philosophical introduction, important when transposing to Portuguese and very French art, although it does not manifest itself in France[41].

In the work of Mário Eloy (1900-1951) there is an emotional dimension that clashes with the rational and its expression becomes particular due to the contradictory dimension of reason-emotion. In this way, forms are built in tension with emotion, with a critical attitude and subjectivity of the subject acting in the real[42].

In the 1920s, with Dórdio Gomes (1890-1976), expressionism is a stain with gestures, far from the German dimension like Paul Cézanne (1839-1906) and Van Gogh (1853-1890), it is an oscillation between ancha that is built and stains that moves. In Eduardo Afonso Viana (1881-1967), however, the stain excludes expressionism with gestures of construction of the referent and there is concern about the presence of things.

In Mily Podez (1888-1967), the gesture is very lively, sensitive and light, but without dramatic intensity or charge. On the other hand, Stuart Carvalhais (1887-1961) is a Portuguese reference linked to Comics.

In 1927, the first version of the magazine *Presença* was released and, in 1930, the *I Salão dos Independentes* was created and held at the Sociedade Nacional de Belas Artes, in Lisbon[43].

Returning to the figure of Mário Eloy, he appears in the 1920s, without academic training, but was fascinated by the

---

[41] *Cf.* WORRINGER, Wilhelm, *Abstracción y naturaleza*, México, Fondo de Cultura Económica, 1953.

[42] DIAS, *Ecos expressionistas...*, p. 218.

[43] Idem, p. 30.

artistic production of Columbano Bordalo Pinheiro (1857-1929) and Eduardo Afonso Viana (1881-1967).

Eloy begins with the influence of Eduardo Afonso Viana (1881-1967) until Paul Cézanne (1839-1906), both in terms of formal issues, as well as in the color palette[44].

In 1924, he exhibited with Alberto Cardoso, who was one of the first Portuguese artists to go to Paris, as well as Eduardo Afonso Viana and others.

Three years later, he meets António Marques and in this period that Nazism is growing, he returns from Germany with his friend António Ferro (1895-1956) in the power of António Salazar (1889-1970)[45]. The latter sought to oppose the naturalist tradition and the Society of Fine Arts.

On the other hand, at this time there were two prizes, the Columbano Prize, for the ancient moderns and, the Amadeo Prize, for the young fluorescent.

When he returns to Portugal, he uses Pablo Picasso's (1881-1973) production from the 1920s as a reference, and from now on, it is impossible to look at Eloy's work without seeing the material and texture. Another reference, Hein Semke (1899-1995), German expressionist sculpture, based on the art of anti-war domination. In Semke's works, it is possible to observe enormous solidity of the very Roman body and clinging to the block - limit game between the figure and the block is very tense[46].

In fact, Eloy will live in the atelier of Hein Semke and Paulo Pereira, the latter being a painter who works deeply with material as texture and light management. In this way, we will

---

[44] DIAS, *Ecos expressionistas...*, p. 36.

[45] DIAS, *Ecos expressionista...*, p. 215.

[46] *Cf.* SILVEIRA, Miguel de & SEMKE, Hein, *Exposição de escultura e cerâmica de Hein Semke*, Lisboa, Secretariado Nacional de Informação, 1947.

see in Eloy's work these repercussions, where the light serves to create volume for the body and is not exactly an ambient light - it is in the body that the luminous variation is decided.

Summing up Eloy's work, it is based on rationalism, with a twisting tension that creates expressionism, like a game of matter and gesture in search of form[47].

Finally, many of Eloy's works were subjected to examination methods, namely low-light photography and radiography.

Finally, the presentation ended with a brief preview of some works by the following authors: Júlio dos Reis Pereira (1902-1983), Carlos Botelho (1899-1982), Dominguez Alvarez (1906-1942), Sarah Afonso (1899-1983) , Almada Negreiros (1893-1970), Paulo Ferreira (1911-1999), Lino António (1898-1974), among others.

---

[47] DIAS, *Ecos expressionistas...*, pp. 249/250.

Free drawing schools

This theme does not approach drawing from an elitist perspective of artistic training and which falls only on a restricted group of interests: those who attend and those who enjoy, traditionally linked to the nobility and the clergy.

In this way, a gap is created between liberal and mechanical arts. This first one is part of an intellectual training plan, which John Locke is careful to refer to the questions of mechanical art and the usefulness of drawing, and yet, the question of pure artistic teaching (as drawing is useless). As for the mechanical arts, these are linked to the production of machines, with practical application[48].

The same is not true of Jean-Jacques Rousseau (1712-1778), dedicated to drawing with the perspective of knowledge linked to perception (reality that surrounds us), moving away from a rhetoric based on the Academy, with Greco-Roman matrices and training governed by concepts unquestioned[49].

In fact, anatomy and perspective were the basis. What mattered later was to guarantee pure artistic development, with the consecration of what was best in the production of art objects that corresponded to the expectations (decoration of palaces and churches).

The Free Design Schools appear in a parallel plan for the production of decorative arts such as tapestry, ornaments, etc., where training was essential for their workers.

These schools obey not only this lack, but also the certainty that the occupation of young people who finished

---

[48] LEBEN, Ulrich, *Object Design in the Age of Enlightnment*, Los Angeles, The J. Paul Getty Museum, 2005, p. 14.

[49] LEBEN, Ulrich, *L'École Royale Gratuite de Dessin de Paris*, Saint-Rémy-en-l'Eau, Éditions Monelle Hayot, 2004, p. 28.

primary education, many were apprentices in workshops, which guaranteed guidance and contact with educational institutions that required discipline, provision of capacity tests and taking advantage of the financing that was being done (bringing down the idleness)[50].

The difference between the Academy and the Free Design School is based on professional training and its consequent function[51]. In addition to the fact that many teachers from the Free Design Schools came from the Academies, the Free Design School allowed direct work with the decorative arts and, interestingly, the teaching method was used until 1968[52].

In fact, there is a connection with the Enlightenment and Diderot's Encyclopedia, where mentalities were based on 18th century free thought and nationalism[53].

The set of reason and thought results in ideas of free thought, as a vehicle for the transmission of ideas that need the image as a complement to that information. This knowledge, mainly of a scientific nature, required the complementarity of illustration. As an example, Diderot's Encyclopedia itself is saturated with images, to which engraving was essential due to the lack of photography.

Teaching principles are therefore useful. The design was linked to an economic system that was demanding and competitive, where the director of the Free School stated "the product that resulted from the design, valued 100 times". We then have a capitalist system associated with these schools *vis-à-vis* of the *Académie Royale de Peinture*[54].

---

[50] LEBEN, Ulrich & GILLESPIE, Susan, 'New Light on the École Royale Gratuite de Dessin: The Years 1766-1815', in *Studies in the Decorative Arts*, Volume 1, Number 1, 1993, pp. 99-118.

[51] LEBEN, *L'École Royale Gratuite de Dessin...*, pp. 17/18.

[52] LEBEN, *Object Design in the Age...*, p. 14

[53] LEBEN, *L'École Royale Gratuite de Dessin...*, p. 28.

[54] LEBEN, *L'École Royale Gratuite de Dessin...*, p. 43

Contrary to what happens today, the abyss of the Schools of the Arts and the Decorative Schools did not exist in France, since one of the functions is the promotion of the French citizen[55]. The institution allowed to leave the "artisanal" worker to have a status[56].

What is at the base of the teaching of these schools is Geometry, associated with mathematics, with a formative sense and contrary to what the Arts ended up proposing in terms of styles. There is a desire to halt the Rocaille process[57].

This is also because the French were impregnated by reason, unlike the Italian Renaissance with its boldness, the French Renaissance is purely rational.

Before the figures responded to a framing in space with theatricality, but now there are figures in countless positions. The body gains movement and torsion.

On the other hand, there is a tendency to curb whims, a whole production for the Aristocracy - focus of court or luxury pleasure that has nothing to do with these strands of social and educational concern[58].

It is not a teaching based on copy and print, but part of the current reality and real objects. The drawing is oriented towards a better observation and correction of errors. There is a sense of play.

Free Design School Mentors:

- Antoine Ferrand de Monthelor, 1746
- Jean-Baptiste Descamps, 1767
- M. Rozoy, 1769
- Jean Jacques Bachelier, 1766

---

[55] LEBEN, *Object Design in the Age...*, p. 41.
[56] Idem, p. 38.
[57] Idem, p. 42
[58] LEBEN, *L'École Royale Gratuite de Dessin...*, p. 50.

Leresse is famous for the Dutch Poussin and is portrayed by Rembrandt. In the blind period, due to syphilis, a painting and drawing treaty is dictated to his son, in which he consecrates Geometry as the basis of the whole principle of Drawing. On the other hand, in his work he also demonstrates concerns at the pedagogical level, giving indications to teachers: a good student comes from a good teacher.

This perception is part of an ethical aspect. The citizenship project is based on economics and ethics, and Drawing is a vehicle for the transmission of knowledge.

Free Design Schools appear throughout France, with the aim of instructing workers, based teaching on an ethical and labor aspect, allowing intelligent work.

Those who attended these schools were young people between 10 and 12 years old, of diverse social origin, mostly from the geographic origin associated with the location of the School and had the following duties and obligations: respect, discipline, decency and attendance.

In the 19th century, naturalism came to affirm the aesthetics of the ugly, against the corrections of nature and the beautiful ideal. The question of the nude appears as a support for the construction of a painting, through direct observation, contrasting the medieval aesthetics.

Research, transversality and specificity

Research in the arts must focus on new issues and the search for these issues must ask how to look | recognize | fight for | read on | use | imagine things that don't exist.

These questions opened the 31st Bienal de São Paulo (2014) [59] with exhibitions of works that address various languages of contemporary art, such as video, installation, *performance*, etc., and on the other hand, issues around the public of museums and contemporary art institutions were also debated.

Contemporary art hosts several activities, in which the artistic object is defined by dematerialization, where it is often no longer physical material, but rather the order of events and with a transcendent or conceptual existence.

This idea is remote and comes from Francisco de Holanda (1517-1585), when he defines in his work *Da Pintura Antiga* (original of 1548) that the painting is "cosa mentale", operating in the field of ideas[60].

On the one hand, research in art consists of looking for something that we don't even know if it exists and the spirit of this conference was to let it go by something that doesn't exist. In this way, we can define three metaphors: cloud, constellation and nebula. These are giants and there are not enough images to capture them.

About the structure of the doctorate, this includes a curricular plan, where there is the possibility in the second year

---

[59] Available at http://www.31bienal.org.br/ [22-12-2014].

[60] HOLANDA, Francisco de, *Da Pintura Antiga*, Lisboa, Imprensa Nacional, [s.d.] (original de 1548), p. 89-91.
SERRÃO, *A Pintura Maneirista...*, p. 19.

to oppose the investigation with critics and obtain various opinions about the project.

Clark E. Moustakas, in his work *Heuristic research: design, methodology and applications*[61], approaches research in the arts as a narration of the artist's own experience (empiricism), resulting in a personal *modus operandi*.

The way we deal with global and accessible information forces us to relate to the permanent increase in information on any subject. In other words, it is constantly the target of new research and knowledge, in which this expansion is impossible to limit.

In this way, it is necessary to limit our research to knowledge until a certain date, always giving rise to the possibility of new formulations of our project. With this, it is essential to limit the scope of our investigation, in which it must be personal and private.

The articulation between theory and practice must bet on a practical investigation, which is decisive for the theory to be built, always assuming the competences and areas to be investigated. This search for knowledge must be complete and grounded, in a constant relationship between what reaches and what does not arrive as reasons for investigation and research. On the other hand, these relationships play with the personal perspective that is essential for building a project safely.

This heuristic research allows organization of work concepts. Distinguishing the works of Maria Pamplona[62] and Carole Gray & Julian Malins[63].

---

[61] *Cf.* MOUSTAKAS, Clark E., *Heuristic research: design, methodology and applications*, Newbury Park, Sage Pub., 1990.

[62] *Cf.* PAMPLONA, Mª Ángeles, *Investigarte. Andamios para una construcción de la invesstigación en Bellas Artes*, Madrid, Universidade Complutense de Madrid, 2003.

Kim Etherington in his work *Becoming a Reflexive Researcher: Using Our Selves in Research[64]*, gives the self-reflexive search importance and essential to support the subjective self-intrusion in the investigation, referring to the investigation diary as a fundamental part of a quality project.

Daniel Danétis in his work *Pratiques artistiques et pratiques de recherche[65]*, relates research practices to artistic practice.

Gary Knowles and Ardra Cole with their work *Handbook of the Arts in Qualitative Research: Perspectives, Methodologies, Examples and Issues[66]*, emerges as antagonism to quantitative research (for example, research in science), where it is based more on quality criteria than quantity[67]. This qualitative research lives on networks of authors and systems by analogy and not cause-effect.

Steven Henry Madoff in his work *Art school (propositions for the 21st century)[68]* displays a compilation of texts dedicated to artistic research in an academic context.

James Elkins in his work *Artists with PhDs (On the new Doctoral Degree in Studio Art)[69]*, addresses the issues

---

[63] *Cf.* GRAY, Carole & MALINS, Julian, *Visualizing Research: A Guide To The Research Process In Art And Design*, London, Ashgate Pub Ltd, 2004.

[64] *Cf.* ETHERINGTON, Kim, *Becoming a Reflexive Researcher: Using Our Selves in Research*, London, Jessica Kingsleu Pub., 2004.

[65] *Cf.* DANÉTIS, Daniel, *Pratiques artistiques et pratiques de recherche*, Paris, L'Harmattan, 2007.

[66] *Cf.* KNOWLES, Gary & COLE, Ardra, *Handbook of the Arts in Qualitative Research: Perspectives, Methodologies, Examples and Issues*, London, Sage Pub., 2007.

[67] BARRETT, Estelle & BOLT, Barbara, *Practice as Research: Approaches to Creative Arts Enquiry*, London, I.B. Tauris & Co Ltd., 2010, pp. 150/151.

[68] *Cf.* MADOFF, Steven Henry, *Art school (propositions for the 21st century)*, London, M.I.T. Press, 2009.

surrounding the doctorate in the studio, that is, the artist who investigates on his own production.

Katy Macleod with her work *Thinking Through Art: Reflections on Art as Research (Innovations in Art and Design)*[70] and the contribution with *Writing and the PhD in fine art*[71], they represent two reference works, whose methodologies for reflecting on artistic practice make it possible to support research bases in doctoral contexts.

The artistic turn: A Manifesto by Katheleen Coessens is a work more linked to research in the area of music, but whose methodology can be applied to other artistic areas[72].

John Freeman elaborated the work *Blood Sweat and Theory: Research Through Practice in Performance (Music + Performing Arts)*[73], addressing research questions related to the performing arts. On the other hand, Baz Kershaw & Helen Nicholoson link theater and performance, addressing methodological and singular aspects in this type of art[74].

---

[69] *Cf.* ELKINS, James, *Artists wirh PhDs (On the new Doctoral Degree in Studio Art)*, Washington DC, New Academia, 2009.

[70] *Cf.* MACLEOD, Katy, *Thinking Through Art: Reflections on Art as Research (Innovations in Art and Design)*, London, Routledge, 2009.

[71] *Cf.* MACLEOD, Katy & HOLDRIDGE, Lin, 'Writing and the PhD in fine art', in *The Routledge companion to research in the arts*, New York, Routledge, 2010, pp. 353-367.

[72] *Cf.* COESSENS, Katheleen, *The artistic turn: A Manifesto (Orphues Research Centre in Music Series ORCiM)*, Leuven, Leuven University Press, 2009.

[73] *Cf.* FREEMAN, John, *Blood Sweat and Theory: Research Through Practice in Performance (Music + Performing Arts)*, Oxford, Libri Publishing, 2010.

[74] *Cf.* KERSHAW, Baz & NICHOLSON, Helen, *Research Methods in Theatre and Performance (Research Methods for the Arts and Humanities)*, Edinburgh, Edinburgh University Press, 2010.

James Daichendt focuses on issues of artistic and literary research[75], while Henk Borgdorff elaborates the work *The Conflict of the Faculties: Perspectives on Artistic Research and Academia*[76], discussing artistic issues and academic demands, admitting it as its great difficulty.

Michael Biggs & Henrik Karlsson is a reference work, covering different themes and methodologies applied to the arts[77].

Estelle Barrett and Barbara Bolt present their own methodology, whose order of investigation should be: state of the art, state of the art, methodology, exegesis (discussion of practice in the studio) and, finally, discussion and reflection on meanings[78].

The performance and research paradigm is based on the various levels of approximation possible to be accomplished through different methods, such as the scientific, multidisciplinary and artistic procedural method. Within the possible practices, these can be empirical, interpretive or even practical. However, it is difficult to establish closed lines of research, whose timing is possible, but it must be flexible to carry out design reformulations.

This open and advocated strategy by Barrett & Bolt[79], is based on the following points:

- Preliminary mapping;

---

[75] *Cf.* DAICHENDT, James, *Artist Scholar: Reflections on Writing and Research,* Bristol, Intellect Ltd, 2011.

[76] *Cf.* BORGDORFF, Henk, *The Conflict of the Faculties: Perspectives on Artistic Research and Academia,* Leiden, Leiden University Press, 2012.

[77] *Cf.* BIGGS, Michael, KARLSSON, Henrik, *The Routledge Companion to Research in the Arts (Routledge Companions),* London, Routledge, 2012.

[78] *Cf.* BARRETT & BOLT, *op. cit.,* 2010.

[79] Ibidem.

- o Central issues;
- o Possible structures (concept maps).
- o State of the Art;
- o In the artistic field;
- o Theory and frame of reference.
- Methodology;
  - o In the artistic process;
  - o In the more theoretical investigation process;
  - o In the writing process.

- Exegesis.
  - o Analysis and interpretation of the body of artistic work;
  - o Permanent relationship with theorization;
  - o "Merciless" criticism for a more objective articulation and evaluation of the work done with innovative knowledge production.

In the doctoral thesis, poetic analogies and metaphors should be avoided, although it is sometimes necessary to resort to creative writing to embody something that does not exist. On the other hand, the design of conceptual maps is an essential tool for organizing ideas.

In this way, we can distinguish the following possible phases in the investigation: analysis, mapping and personal assessment of objectives; identification of the question - hypothesis, formulation and summary; state of the art; structure (open, auxiliary use of heuristic maps); research and investigation - readings, data collection and doing (art and writing); constant organization and reorganization, scheduling and *recalendarization*; written evaluation; and elaboration of the next program.

The opening with a quote by Frederico Fellini and his film E la nave va (1983), allows us to idealize the painting of our day as a phoenix that is permanently dying and being born from its own ashes.

Fellini dreamed of the death of cinema via television and the media. In this film, Fellini crude what cinema surpasses. In fact, it exists as an artistic object, where the sea itself is artificial.

The parallelism with painting, apparently closed in on itself, demonstrates an enormous openness of the arts and enters the cultural industries - mass society and the need to entertain the spectator.

In this way, museums are also widespread, both in closed spaces, as street arts museums, etc.

In Hubert Damisch's A Theory of cloud, it is possible to find a comparative history of painting as a discourse in other domains, creating a paradigm in the history of painters[80]. In fact, the painting has a carbonated profile and the cloud represents a symptom.

Through the works of Alexander Cozens (1717-1786), William Turner (1775-1851) and René Magritte (1898-1967), we can observe that painting increasingly detaches itself from the real, passing its attention to what is fleeting.

In Hubert Damisch's work, painting is described as a pulverized development, strongly represented by Impressionism, whose relationship with the visible is discredited to give shape to the invisible and the unconscious that has no determined form, but is codified.

Olafur Eliasson (1967-) defines his work as painting expanded to space, between genres, gestures or actions such as

---

[80] Cf. DAMISCH, Hubert, A Theory of Cloud: toward a history of painting, Stanford, Stanford University Press, 2002.

Wheather Project[81]. On the other hand, Cai Zhisong's (1972-) installation held at the Chinese Pavilion at the 54th Venice International Biennial (Italy), entitled Cloud, consisted of a device that released water vapor. Or even, the work of Tomás Saraceno (1973-), with the work *On Space Time Foam*[82], it is also an installation that generates a paradigm that has always existed as experiencing the lack of gravity, a question permanently explored by man.

Other artists still like Kohei Nawa (1975-[83], Anish Kapoor (1954-)[84], Caitlind Brown (1961-)[85], or the playful works of Berndnaut Smilde (1978-), *Nimbus*, which results in the creation of artificial situations, and in this case, the creation of clouds that remain present for a short time.

In fact, after Marcel Duchamp (1887-1968), reflections on art have been carried out around the path and evolution of contemporary art, and also, as the public has determined the artistic device[86]. On the other hand, contemporary production is often so widespread that private institutions turn to art to entertain the masses.

Thus, there is a need to build a critical device.

---

[81] Available at http://www.tate.org.uk/whats-on/exhibition/unilever-series-olafur-eliasson-weather-project/olafur-eliasson-weather-project [22-12-2014].

[82] Available at http://www.tomassaraceno.com/MET/Bicocca/ [22-12-2014].

[83] Available at http://www.kohei-nawa.net/ [22-12-2014].

[84] Available at http://anishkapoor.com/ [22-12-2014].

[85] Available at http://incandescentcloud.com/about-the-artist-2/ [22-12-2014].

[86] *Cf.* DUVE, Thierry de, *Kant after Duchamp*, Cambridge, M.I.T. Press, 1996.

ROBERTS, John, *The Intangibilities of Form: Skill and Deskilling in Art after the Readymade*, London, Verso, 2007.

In metaphorical terms, Man Ray (1890-1976), with his photography *Dust Breeding* (1920) will appropriate a work by Marcel Duchamp (1887-1968), entitled *The Bride Stripped Bare by Her Bacherlors Even*, to record the status and remain as work in progress.

The dust recorded by Man Ray is a metaphor like anything strange. George Bataille, in his text *Dust*[87], he wonders what it would be like if Snow White, as long as she was asleep, woke up full of dust, or even the idea of the number of women who clean dust every day and the closed books that they try to share their knowledge with.

On the other hand, dust by means of pigments, as paints used to do until the 18th century, when they started to be produced industrially and in the 19th century were placed in paint tubes. Thierry de Duve also considers the paint tube to be the first ready-made because this paint tube contains a possible painting[88].

Also in Cesare Ripa we have another metaphor, the beauty metaphor, in which it is related to what is not seen and is sometimes hidden[89].

Thus, also in Fellini's film, the rhino is a metaphor for the unconscious, whose artistic project he invokes in his heart and needs to be safe.

---

[87] BATAILLE, George et al., 'Dust', in *Encyclopaedia Acephalica (Atlas Arkhive)*, London, Atlas Press, pp. 42/43.

[88] DUVE, Thierry de, 'The Readymade and the Tube of Paint: Marcel Duchamp, Still Unraveling', in *Artforum*, Volume 24, Number 9, 1986, pp. 110-121.

[89] *Cf.* RIPA, Cesare, *Iconologia: overo descrittione di diverse imagini cavate dall'antichità*, Hildesheim, Georg Olms, 2003.

VENABLE, Bradford, 'The"Iconologia": Helping Art Students Understand Allegory', in *Art Education*, Volume 61, Number 3, 2008, pp. 15-21.

Physical investigation of pigments

Dividing into 6 points: **1.** What is the importance of identifying the pigments; **2.** FRX; **3.** Spectrometer; **4.** Interpret XRF spectra of pigments; **5.** Characterization *in situ* and 6. Conclusion.

1. The identification and characterization of the pigments used in works allows to know the author's palette, to date by comparison when comparing with other works studied from the same period, to indicate the state of conservation and also, allows to carry out an expert examination (identification of false ones)[90].

To exemplify what was being given, the example of the famous Vermeer forger - Han van Meegeren - was given, whose expert process was based on the identification of the element cobalt (Co) in blue (cobalt blue), which appeared only in the 19th century[91]. Bearing in mind that Johannes Vermeer is a 17th century Flemish painter, this pigment did not yet exist, but the ultramarine blue, which was the painter's favorite blue pigment[92].

With this example it was possible to perceive the applicability of the X-ray fluorescence technique, also being given as an example, still on the production of this counterfeiter,

---

[90] GÓMEZ, Maria Luisa, *La restauración: Examen científico aplicado a la conservación de obras de arte*, Madrid, Catedra-Cuadernos Arte, 2008, pp. 147-156.

[91] COVEY, Preston K., 'Art or Forgery? The Strange Case of Han Van Meegeren', in *The Journal of Computing in Higher Education*, Volume 2, Number 1, 1990, p. 2-31.

[92] See more at http://www.nationalgallery.org.uk/paintings/research/meaning-of-making/vermeer-and-technique/vermeers-palette [20-01-2015].

the absence of silver (Ag) and antimony (Sb), impurities present in lead white, given the manual production of this pigment[93].

The famous case of conservation of Van Gogh's paintings was also given as an example, namely the absence of a protective layer, characteristic of impressionist painters, which would prove to be a degradation medium to the yellow cadmium pigment, easily oxidizable[94]. In this way, the yellow cadmium pigment, with enormous chromatic strength, is lost to a whitish tone, changing the plastic and aesthetic reading of the work.

This demonstrates the importance of knowing the pigments present in the works to decide the best conservation method. In these terms, as is the case with cadmium yellow, knowing that this pigment is photosensitive, it will be necessary to preserve the works with this compound in a low light environment.

On the other hand, the example of tattoos was also given, in the United States of America, there is no legislation on the use of applied pigments, and in this way, pigments can contain dyes or heavy metals. The case of permanent makeup can also demonstrate adverse effects and allergies.

2. The X-ray fluorescence technique consists of an elementary analysis technique (identification of elements with

---

[93] Forgery. Dutchman who painted Vermeers. Available at http://webartacademy.com/forgery-dutchman-who-painted-vermeers [15-12-2014].

[94] MONICO, Letizia et al., 'Degradation Process of Lead Chromate in Paintings by Vincent van Gogh Studied by Means of Synchrotron X-Ray Spectromicroscopy and Related Materials. 2. Original Paint Layer Samples', in *Analytical Chemistry*, Volume 83, Number 4, pp. 1224-1231.

Idem, 'Degradation Process of Lead Chromate in Paintings by Vincent van Gogh Studied by Means of Synchrotron X-Ray Spectromicroscopy and Related Materials. 3. Synthesis, Characterization and Detection of Different Crystal Forms of the Chrome Yellow Pigment', in *Analytical Chemistry*, Volume 85, Number 2, pp. 851-859.

an atomic number greater than 12 - magnesium) that allows simultaneous identification in the sample, being qualitative and quantitative (if it is a gold alloy). One of the great advantages of this technique is its fast, non-destructive and non-invasive approach, being in some cases a very portable device (Bruker pistol).

The discoverer of X radiation was Wilhelm Röentgen (1845-1923), discharging energy into an ampoule, but as it was not possible to observe anything with the naked eye, he placed an aluminum foil and a barium salt card at the end of the ampoule, making it possible observe fluorescence with this radiation[95].

On the other hand, he also realized that this radiation penetrated different materials. Then, with his wife's hand, he took the first X-ray.

The principle of the X-ray fluorescence technique is to use an X radiation source to ionize the innermost layers of atoms. When an X-ray photon is placed on a sample, it will pull an atom from the innermost layer, creating a gap. As all matter naturally seeks to return to its fundamental state, an atom from an outermost layer will transition to that layer, emitting a photon corresponding to the difference in energies of these two layers. This resulting photon is detected and processed in the form of a spectrum.

4. In this spectrum, the position of the peaks, read on the abscissa, allows the identification of the elements (from the periodic table) present in the sample. The number of counts for each peak, read in the ordinate, allows determining the quantity of each element present in a sample / object.

---

[95] TOLEDO-PEREYRA, Luis H., 'X-Ray Surgical Revolution', in *Journal of Investigative Surgery*, Volume 22, Issue 5, pp. 327-332.

This objective peak / element reading is universally consultable in databases with a numbering system (nomenclature) such as Siegbahn and IUPAC[96].

Then, a list of pigments and an energy table were provided. Regarding the intensity ratio of these peaks, the one corresponding to the streak K is always higher than L. On the other hand, it is necessary to pay attention to the use of the linear scale for reading a spectrum, since it can mask peaks of lesser intensity.

This technique was compared with Raman spectroscopy that was not addressed in terms of its foundation and practice. In fact, it is indicated by a laptop, but it presents itself as transportable and slow, considering the X-ray fluorescence technique. On the other hand, a work of art placed under the lens of a microscope attached to Raman spectroscopy equipment is not always possible. This technique makes use of monochromatic and intense radiation, being more complicated and less rapid, requiring greater care with cultural assets[97].

3. As for the spectrometer, there are both laboratory and portable, allowing mapping quickly. Recently, applications of this technique using a pistol have been recurrent (Bruker®), differentiating itself by the quality of the spectrum obtained. However, the portability of this technique allows studies *in situ*[98], laboratory equipment allows to obtain results with higher quality.

5. The *in situ* characterization was a practical work carried out at the end of the session. The first object analyzed was a fragment of parchment with blue and red ink (undated), the first point of analysis being in a red area (analyzing pigment, preparation and parchment). Before analyzing this fragment, the

---

[96] Fonte: http://old.iupac.org/reports/V/spectro/partVIII.pdf [13-12-2014].

[97] Risk of burning or losing samples.

[98] Whenever it is not possible to remove the work from its environment.

calibration process was explained, constituting itself through the analysis of samples with known elements. After calibration, the fragment was analyzed and the element mercury (Hg) was identified, indicating the presence of vermilion. This pigment had been widely used in the making of manuscripts. It was also possible to identify the presence of calcium (Ca), linked to the preparation of the parchment. On the other hand, in the blue zone, it was possible to identify copper (Cu) and zinc (Zn), with copper being able to indicate the presence of the azurite pigment. In this case, it is necessary to resort to contextualization with the time of the work, using the bibliography. Finally, a blue and white tile was also analyzed, having identified the element cobalt (Co), indicative of the blue pigment of cobalt, and also lead (Pb) and zirconium (Zr), characteristic of the glaze.

6. This technique allows to identify the composition of elements present in artistic objects, being non-destructive and does not require removal of the sample. On the other hand, it allows answering questions of execution, constituting valuable information for the conservation and restoration, as well as the study of degradation processes, or even falsification.

The conservator can use this information to build the treatment methodology, allowing better prevention choices to be made.

Contemporary Museology

On the practice of museology, Nuno Sacramento's work was referenced and the issues of museology reaching the community[99]. That is, it is necessary to leave the museum and work with communities, raising questions related to Anthropology, Communication and approach to Education, where Educational Services have been growing[100].

The challenges of Museology are linked to the research methodology and for students who carry out theses in this area it is essential to start writing the thesis right from the beginning. Within the methodology, the role of the advisor is fundamental to assist in asking questions and distinctions between main and secondary questions.

On the other hand, but still regarding the research methodology, the difference between case studies and examples was pointed out, the first being indicated as complex and based on multiple dimensions systems, where it is possible to draw knowledge[101].

In a second part of the class, issues related to change in museums were discussed, dividing these issues into two groups: external and internal causes. In this first group, we can point out communication issues and their relationship with new

---

[99] SACRAMENTO, Nuno, 'Artocracy: art, informal space, and social consequente ou simplesmente "far from reality"', in *Arte & Sociedade*, Lisboa, 2011, pp. 416-429.

[100] MAIO, Fernanda, '" Vidas reais, gente real": A re-presentação de outros na arte no espaço público', in *Revista Crítica de Ciências Sociais*, Número 75, 2006, pp. 95-115.

[101] ECO, Humberto, *Como se faz uma tese em ciências humanas*, Lisboa, Presença, 1988, pp. 65-69.

technologies [102] . In fact, some museums have become repositories of works, with permanent collections that do not rotate, etc. [103], freezing in the evolutionary time proper to museology and its historical accompaniment.

In the second group, it is possible to point out the fact that the temporary exhibitions do not contain works from the museum, these same exhibitions being a survival factor of a museum institution[104]. On the other hand, museum management is a factor in the sustainability of the museum, giving as an example the importance of the community having knowledge and understanding of the money spent in a museum.

Institutional criticism represents a true bourgeois vanguard that changes in the 60s to turn against the museum itself [105]. The example of the artists who went on "strike" in relation to museums is given because it had the right to exhibit and artists no longer had a say in their own production.

On the other hand, some artists began to intervene in their own works, with a new look at the collection, revisiting history in a new perspective. In this way, museums that did not fight against institutional criticism ended up dignifying themselves and changing their course to new paradigms that can still be visited today.

---

[102] SHANKEN, Edward A., 'Art in the Information Age: Technology and Conceptual Art', in Leonardo, Volume 35, Number 4, 2002, pp. 433-438.

GIGLIOTTI, Carol, 'Bridge to, Bridge from: The Arts, Technology and Education', in Leonardo, Volume 31, Number 2, 1998, pp. 89-92.

[103] The Gulbenkian Museum was given as an example. Interestingly, this museum already includes a virtual tour platform. Available at http://museu.gulbenkian.pt/Museu/pt/Museu/VisitaVirtual [12-01-2015].

[104] JONES, Peter, 'Museums and the Meanings of Their Contents', in New Literary History, Volume 23, Number 4, 1992, pp. 911-921.

[105] WARD, Frazer, 'The Haunted Museum: Institutional Critique and Publicity', in October, Volume 73, 1995, pp. 71-89.

Other issues raised in this session, and with enormous relevance, were the significance of the collections that are based on ideology and politics, as well as globalization and its fight with culture[106]. In this last point, the reflection on simultaneous times at the same time, characteristic of postmodernism, was provoked.

Still on issues of museological sustainability, the example of the USA was given, whose museums seek funding through patronage and can enjoy policies for buying and selling works from their collection[107]. Thus, it strengthens the collection and captivates the public that never tires of seeing the same museum due to the exhibition rotation.

At the end of the session, it was possible to point out several factors that can enhance museological institutions, such as, for example, the museum's space being used to conserve, educational services aimed at children, Merchandising and museum and community. All the issues raised constitute a narrative that seeks to meet cultural complexity.

---

[106] *Cf.* URRY, John, *The Tourist Gaze*, London, Sage, 2001.

KIRSHENBLATT-GIMBLETT, Barbara, *Destination Culture. Tourism, Museums and Heritage*. Berkeley, University of California Press, 1998.

[107] LEWIS, Geoffry, 'The Role of Museums and the Professional Code of Ethics', in *Runninf a Museum: A Practical Handbook*, Paris, ICOM, pp. 1-16.

Exposure as material and relational practice

At the time of the Enlightenment, where education became democratic and universal, collecting began to have a direct relationship with the bourgeoisie and became involved in education[108]. The great example is the *Encyclopédie* by Diderot, consisting of a true State of the art of the knowledge of the time[109].

In the 18th and 19th centuries, major exhibitions such as the Salons, created first connections with museums, despite having a jury and being directly linked to academics[110].

The exhibition differs from the exhibition in that it is a public presentation of objects of cultural interest[111], including value for that audience and focusing on a particular space. On the other hand, it requires interpretation and the object itself has curatorial practice, framing in space and creates an interface with the public - which implies a method.

---

[108] MICHEL, Régis & WRIGLEY, Richard, 'Diderot and Modernity', in *Oxford Art Journal*, Volume 8, Number 2, 1985, pp. 36-51.

[109] *Cf.* DIDEROT, Denis, ALEMBERT, Jean Le Rond d'& MOUCHON, Pierre, *Encyclopédie*, Paris, Briasson, 1751. Available at https://archive.org/details/encyclopdieoudi03alemgoog [15-12-2014].

[110] *Cf.* DIDEROT, Denis, *Essais sur la peinture: salons de 1759, 1761, 1763*, Paris, Hermann, 1984.
Idem, *Salon de 1765*, Paris, Hermann, 1984.

[111] *Cf.* GRAY, Carole & MALINS, Julian , *Visualizing Research: A Guide to the Research Process in Art and Design*, Oxford, Ashgate, 2004.
LYONS, Lucy, 'Walls Are Not My Friends: Issues Surrounding the Dissemination of Practice-led Research within Appropriate and Relevant Contexts', in *Working Papers in Art and Design*, Number 4, 2006. Available at https://www.herts.ac.uk/__data/assets/pdf_file/0003/12387/WPIAAD_v ol4_ lyons.pdf [12-01-2015].

The function of the exhibition, as an exhibition, is to make different objects from the museological or private collections visible, which in general are not on display.

The public scenario is based on location, montage and narrative, and has an important role that, despite being artificial, has a social discourse. This speech can have different points of view and therefore, different strategies to approach the public.

In 1787, with the Louvre or the Salons, the paintings were displayed from the floor to the ceiling and are practical until the beginning of the 20th century[112]. At this time there is no concern in the way of exhibiting the works.

The imaginary world comes into being insofar as the objects inserted on display come to have meaning that they did not have[113]. On the other hand, the title is also important because it denotes a significant character and represents a fundamental element of marketing. These must be assertive, clear and concrete.

An exhibition is the result of manipulation and if, on the one hand, live artists work (for example, anthologically), it is much more complex and difficult to work on the work of deceased authors who require a lot of research work (inside and outside the institution).

The exhibitions often only give a read to the public, such as the Frida Kahlo exhibition in Lisbon, the information was single-celled and not varied (anachronistic).

Exhibitions can have several functions:

1. Symbolic (religious or political glorification);

2. Commercial (commodity value);

---

[112] MCCLELLAN, Andrew L., 'The Musée du Louvre as Revolutionary Metaphor During the Terror', in *The Art Bulletin*, Volume 1, Number 2, 1988, pp. 300-313.

[113] WARD, Martha, 'Impressionist Installations and Private Exhibitions', in *The Art Bulletin*, Volume 73, Number 4, pp. 599-622.

3. Documentary (informative);

4. Aesthetics (artistic value).

These functions are not excluded and can all be in the same exhibition.

The presentation forms allow to characterize exhibition types: permanent, temporary, mobile, mobile and portable.

Temporary agencies are often used to create dialogues between museums and contemporary artists, as well as to motivate the public.

On the other hand, we have characteristics of the works according to the materials: original objects, reproductions, virtual and mixed.

Exhibitions can have a character:

1) Thematic development

2) Thesis

3) Contextualized exhibition

Within these, they can be: 1) Generic; 2) Monographic, 3) Multipurpose; 4) Specials and 5) General historical function.

And further subdivide into:

1) Emotional

2) didactic

3) Playful

4) Others - interactive, participatory, etc.

The social function of art rests on the curator / exhibitor, in cultural centers and museums. The curators can be independent (freelancer and with great essay production) or institutional (group of commentators and with less essay production). In the latter case, curators have a role as institutional decision-makers and work closely with policy and financing.

Institutional purchases and exhibitions are important to the artist's curriculum and it is often scandalous that they ask the artist for a work in exchange.

Contemporary art is based on the dealer, collector and investor, in play with the critical curator, editor and researcher.

Research topics in arts education

It is possible to carry out two different paths in this research area: a) Case studies or b) History of teaching.

Both possibilities of study are recent in Portugal, but research based on case studies has more followers due to the originality - no two cases are the same.

On the other hand, this type of research becomes easier for most researchers, as they are already in educational institutions - they investigate the area they already know and their own students (which is what Umberto Eco advocates[114]). The fact that there is an identification of the person who investigates (observer of the activity of a teacher) can affect the partiality and scientific validity of the investigation. On the other hand, the researcher must be ethical and moral[115].

The starting point of the investigation is the identification of the problem or issue. On the other hand, the thesis represents the beginning of the route (s) rather than the end of the route.

Before the field observation in Artistic Education, it is necessary to carry out the State of the Art for a better data collection. This field observation must be accompanied by a field notebook and can focus on a specific group of students (one or two children with special educational needs, economic factors, emotional stability, etc.), a class, a teacher, several teachers, etc.

It may be interesting to study the "opposite" to cross data, helping the way to the truth. Still on the truth, when making contacts with people, one must consider the susceptibility of

---

[114] *Cf.* ECO, *op. cit.*, 1988.

[115] TUSA, Erzsébet, 'Art Education, or the Art of Education', in *Studia Musicologica Academiae Scientiarum Hungaricae*, Volume 25, Issues 1-4, 1983, pp. 101-109.

failures or untruths, bad intentions, or even the age that can lead to memory failures or confusions.

An interesting question about the investigation is the fact that one cannot be concerned with what is obtained (or not) different from what is said. On the other hand, an unusual case study can help to understand typical or normal non-visible issues that go unnoticed.

This should always aim to improve or advance the background research, even if it is a small step.

The most important thing in qualitative research is interpretation and there are always initial questions that change after observation - progressive focusing[116]. On the other hand, it is not enough to just observe, it is necessary to anticipate through the State of the Art, always starting from a hypothesis.

The investigation consists of the following mode:

Observation -> Hypotheses -> Research -> Conclusions

In which a good thesis always starts from good initial questions. This methodology must use sensitivity and skepticism to question and limit results, as well as having a work plan to help systematize research throughout the PhD. On the other hand, it is essential to create several copies in physical and digital format (backup) of the work that is being developed.

Without neglecting the most important in field research, it is necessary to guarantee access and authorizations. The investigator must not "disappear", he must have good manners and keep promises.

---

[116] Definição de 'Progressive focusing B12', Available at
http://education.illinois.edu/CIRCE/EDPSY49
0E/B12.pdf [12-01-2015].

PARLETT, Malcolm & HAMILTON, David, 'Evaluation as Illumination: A New Approach to the Study of Innovative Programmes', in *Evaluation Studies Review Anual*, Volume 1, 1976, pp. 140-157.

In the case of the History of Art Education, the State of Art constitutes the historical construction - if there is no history, there is no State of Art. Even so, it allows to know what has already been investigated and what remains to be investigated.

Finally, several national and international works related to the History of Artistic Teaching, by authors such as Nikolaus Pevsner[117], Paulino Montez[118], Betâmio de Almeida[119], Saulo Araújo[120], Maria Helena Lisboa[121], Margarida Calado[122] and Miguel Faria[123].

---

[117] *Cf.* PEVSNER, Nikolaus, *Le academie d'art*, Torino, Giulio Einaudi Editore, 1982.

[118] *Cf.* MONTEZ, Paulino, 'Do ensino de Belas Artes em Portugal através dos séculos', in *Boletim da Escola Superior de Belas Artes de Lisboa*, Número 2, 1960, pp. 9-26.

[119] *Cf.* ALMEIDA, Betâmio de, 'Ensino das Artes Plásticas', in *Dicionário de História de Portugal*, Volume II, Porto, Livraria Figueirinhas, 1999.

[120] *Cf.* ARAÚJO, Saulo, *Artífice ou artista?: Uma problemática que acompanha o ensino superior em Portugal no século XIX*, Dissertação de Mestrado em Teorias da Arte, Faculdade de Belas-Artes da Universidade de Lisboa, Lisboa, 2002.

[121] *Cf.* LISBOA, Maria Helena, *As academias e escolas de Belas Artes e o ensino artístico (1836-1910)*, Lisboa, Edições Colibri, 2007.

[122] *Cf.* CALADO, Maria Marques & CALADO, Maria Margarida, *Desenhos dos Séculos XIX e XX - Escola Superior de Belas-Artes de Lisboa*, Lisboa, Escola Superior de Belas Artes de Lisboa, 1975.

Idem, 'Academia do Nu', In PEREIRA, José Fernandes (Ed.) *Dicionário da Arte Barroca em Portugal*, Lisboa, Editorial Presença, 1989.

Idem, 'Ensino', In PEREIRA, José Fernandes (Ed.) *Dicionário da Arte Barroca em Portugal*, Lisboa, Editorial Presença,1989.

Idem, *O Convento de S. Francisco da Cidade. Subsídios para uma Monografia*, Lisboa, Faculdade de Belas-Artes da Universidade de Lisboa, 2011.

Idem, 'Desenhar o corpo - uma metodologia de ensino constante na arte ocidental', In TAVARES, Cristina Azevedo (Ed.) *Representações do corpo na ciência e na arte*, Fim de Século, Lisboa, 2011, pp. 109-124.

CALADO, Margarida & FERRÃO, Hugo, 'Da Academia à Faculdade de Belas Artes', in NÓVOA, António (Ed.), *A Universidade de Lisboa nos* séculos *XIX* e *XX*, Lisboa, Tinta da China, 2013, Vol. II, pp. 1107-1151.

[123] *Cf.* FARIA, Miguel, *O ensino das Belas Artes em Portugal nas vésperas da fundação da Academia*, Lisboa, Universidade Autónoma de Lisboa, 2000.

Themes and modes of investigation in art history

Carl Argan divides Art History into four areas: formalist, sociological, iconological and semiological or structuralist[124]. Laurie Adams, on the other hand, divides into: formalist, iconographic, cultural, biographical, semiotic and psychoanalytic approach, creating a methodology that helps the reading, definition and understanding of works of art[125].

Anne D'Allena will further subdivide each Art History study group, sub-categorizing with areas divided by the previous author[126]. However, Jean Luc Chalumeau simplifies again in the field of Art Theory, dividing it into just: formalism, structural analysis, sociology of art, psychology of art and phenomenology of art[127].

Iconography and iconology were developed by Aby Warburg (1866-1929)[128] and later by Erwin Panofsky (1892-1968)[129]. The study of artistic contexts started from the theories

---

[124] ARGAN, Giulio Carlo, *Guia de história da arte*, Lisboa, Editorial Estampa, 1992, pp. 34-40.

[125] *Cf.* ADAMS, Laurie, *The Methodologies of Art, an introduction,* New York, Icon Editions, 1996.

[126] *Cf.* D'ALLEVA, Anne, *Methods & Theories of Art History*, London, Laurence King Publishing, 2005.

[127] *Cf.* CHAMULEAU, Jean Luc, *As teorias da arte: filosofia, crítica e história da arte: de Platão aos nossos dias*, Lisboa, Instituto Piaget, 1997.

[128] *Cf.* WARBURG, Aby, *Atlas Mnemosyne*, Madrid, Akal D.L., 2010.

[129] *Cf.* PANOFSKY, Erwin, *Significado nas artes visuais*, São Paulo, Perspectiva, 1979.

of Karl Marx (1818-1883), who reflected on the role of art in society early in his career[130].

Semiology was started by Ferdinand de Saussure (1857-1913) [131] and developed by Charles Peirce (1839-1914) [132], Merleau-Ponty (1908-1961)[133] and finally, less quoted, Meyer Schapiro (1904-1996) with huge connection to Marxism [134]. Finally, in the field of psychology and perception we have authors such as Sigmund Freud (1856-1039)[135], Jacques Lacan (1901-1981) [136] and then Ernst Gombrich (1909-2001) and Rudolf Arnheim (1904-2007).

Giorgio Vasari (1511-1674) can be considered the first art historian with his biographical compilation treatise by several authors of the time, entitled *Vite de 'più eccellenti pittori, scultori e architettori* (original edition of 1550)[137].

---

[130] WERCKMEISTER, Otto Karl, 'Marx on Idealogy and Art', in *New Literary History*, Volume 4, Number 3, 1973, pp. 501-519.

LIFSHITZ, M., *The Philosophy of Art of Karl Marx*, New York, Critics Group, 1938, p. 24.

[131] *Cf.* SAUSSURE, Ferdinand de, *Curso de linguística geral*, Lisboa, Dom Quixote, 1992.

[132] *Cf.* PEIRCE, Charles Sanders, *Semiótica*, São Paulo, Pespectiva, 1977.

[133] *Cf.* MERLEAU-PONTY, Maurice, *Fenomenologia da percepção*, São Paulo, Martins Fontes, 1994.

[134] CHAPIRO, Meyer, 'Style', in *Anthropology Today: An Encyclopedia Inventory*, Ed. KRÖBER, A. L., Chicago, University of Chicago Press, 1953, pp. 287-312.

WILLIAMS, John, 'Meyer Schapiro in Silos: Pursuing an Iconography of Style', in *The Art Bulletin*, Volume 85, Number 3, 2003, pp. 442-468.

[135] *Cf.* FREUD, Sigmund, *Essais de psychanalyse*, Paris, Payot, 1979. Idem, *A interpretação dos sonhos*, Lisboa, Relógio de Água, 2009.

[136] *Cf.* LACAN, Jacques, *O seminário*, Rio de Janeiro, Jorge Zahar Editor, 1995.

[137] *Cf.* VASARI, Giorgio, *Le vite de' piú eccellenti pittori, scultori e architettori*, Novara, Istituto Geografico de Agostini, 1967.

However, Johann Winckelmann (1717-1768) is the creator of art history as we know it[138], as well as other later names of international art historiography such as Henirich Wölfflin (1864-1945)[139] and Erwin Panofky (1892-1968).

In the Portuguese case, we can consider Francisco de Holanda (1517-1585) the first Portuguese art historian.

The rest of the session consisted of a very long list of Portuguese authors or those who were in Portugal, with a biographical summary and specific contributions in the field of Art History. The authors presented with reference to the most important literary works are listed: Félix da Costa (1639-1712) [140], José da Cunha Taborda (1766-1816) [141], Cyrillo Volkmar Machado (1748-1823) [142], James Murphy (1760-1814)[143], Conde Athanasius Raczynski (1788-1864)[144], Francisco

[138] *Cf.* WINCKELMANN, Johann Joachim, *Histoire de l'art dans l'antiquité*, Paris, Librarie Génerale Française, 2005.

[139] *Cf.* WÖLFFLIN, Heinrich, *Conceitos fundamentais da História da arte: o problema da evolução dos estilos na arte mais recente*, São Paulo, Martins Fontes, 1984.

[140] *Cf.* COSTA, Félix, *The antiquity of the art of painting*, New Haven, Yale University, 1967.

[141] *Cf.* TABORDA, José da Cunha, *Regras da arte da pintura: com breves reflexões críticas sobre os caracteres distintivos de duas escolas, vidas e quadros de seus mais célebres professores*, Coimbra, Imprensa da Universidade, 1922.

[142] *Cf.* MACHADO, Cyrillo Volkmar, *Collecção de memórias relativas ás vidas dos pintores, e escultores, architectos e gravadores portuguezes, e dos estrangeiros que estiverão em Portugal*, Lisboa, Imprensa de Victorino Rodrigues da Silva, 1823.

[143] *Cf.* SOUSA, Frei Luís de & MURPHY, James Cavanah, *Plans, elevations sections and views of the church of Batalha, in the province of Estremadura in Portugal, with the history and descruption by Fr. Luís de Sousa*, London, Library of Fine Arts, 1836.

[144] *Cf.* RACZNSKI, Le Comte A., *Les Arts en Portugal*, Paris, Jules Renouard et Cie. Libraires-Éditeurs, 1846.

Idem, *Dictionnaire Historico-Artistique du Portugal*, Paris, Jules Renouard et Cie. Libraires-Éditeurs, 1847.

Adolfo de Varnhagen (1816-1878)[145], Almeida Garrett (1799-1854)[146], Alexandre Herculano (1810-1877)[147], Edgar Quinet (1803-1875)[148], Joaquim de Vasconcelos (1849-1936)[149], Alfredo França (1882-1962)[150], Sousa Viterbo (1845-1910)[151], José de Figueiredo (1872-1937)[152], Virgílio Correia (1888-1944)[153], António Nogueira Gonçalves (1901-1998)[154], João Barreira (1866-1961)[155], Reinaldo dos Santos (1880-1970)[156], Eugénio d'Ors (1882-1954)[157], Ernesto Soares (1887-1966)[158], Diogo de

[145] Cf. VARNHAGEN, Adolfo de, *Noticia historica e descriptiva do Mosteiro de Belem*, Lisboa, Typ. Da Sociedade Propagandora dos Conhecimentos Úteis, 1842.

[146] Cf. GARRETT, Almeida, *O retrato de Vénus e Estudos da História Letteraria*, Porto, Viúva Moré, 1867.

[147] Cf. HERCULANO, Alexandre, *Opúsculos: Monumentos Pátrios*, Volume 2, Lisboa, Viúva Bertrand, 1908.

[148] Cf. QUINET, Edgar, *Mes vacances en Espagne*, Paris, Libr. Germer-Bailliére, 1857.

[149] Cf. VASCONCELOS, Joaquim, *Da architectura manuelina*, Coimbra, Imprensa da Universidade, 1885.

[150] Cf. FRANÇA, Alfredo & VALENÇA, Francisco, *Paneleida*, Lisboa, A Peninsular, 1926.

[151] Cf. VITERBO, Sousa, *Noticia de alguns esculptores portuguezes ou que exerceram a sua arte em Portugal*, Lisboa, Typ. Lallement, 1900.
Idem, *Noticia de alguns pintores portuguezes e de outros que, sendo estrangeiros, exerceram a sua arte em Portugal*, Lisboa, Academia Real das Sciencias 1902.

[152] Cf. FIGUEIREDO, José de, *Arte portuguesa primitiva*, Lisboa, [s.n.], 1910.

[153] Cf. CORREIA, Virgílio, *Pintores portugueses dos séculos XV e XVI*, Coimbra, Imprensa da Universidade, 1928.

[154] Cf. GONÇALVES, António Nogueira, *O mestre dos túmulos dos reis*, Coimbra, Faculdade de Letras da Universidade, 1975.

[155] Cf. BARREIRA, João, *Arte portuguesa*, Lisboa, Edições Excelsior, [s.d.].

[156] Cf. SANTOS, Reinaldo dos, *L'art portugais*, Lisbonne, Académie National des Beaux Arts, 1949.

[157] Cf. ORS, Eugénio de, *Du Baroque*, Paris, Gallimard, 1935.

Macedo (1889-1959)[159], Aarão de Lacerda (1890-1947)[160], Mário Tavares Chicó (1905-1966)[161], João Miguel Santos Simões (1907-1972)[162], Adriano de Gusmão (1908-1993)[163], Robert Smith (1912-1975)[164], George Kubler (1912-)[165], Artur Nobre de Gusmão (1920-2001)[166], José-Augusto França (1922-)[167], João Manuel Oleiro (1923-2000)[168], Henrique Pais da Silva (1929-1977)[169], Flávio Gonçalves (1929-1987)[170], Dagoberto Markl (1939-2010)[171], Rafael Moreira (1947-)[172], Vítor Serrão (1952-

[158] Cf. SOARES, Ernesto, *História da gravura artística em Portugal: os artistas e as suas obras*, Lisboa, Samcarlos, 1971.

[159] Cf. MACEDO, Diogo de, *A escultura portuguesa nos séculos XVII e XVIII*, Lisboa, Ocidente, 1945.

[160] Cf. LACERDA, Aarão de, *História da arte em Portugal*, Porto, Portucalense, 1953.

[161] Cf. CHICÓ, Mário Tavares, *Dicionário da Pintura Universal*, 3 Volumes, Lisboa, Estúdios Cor, 1973.

[162] Cf. SIMÕES, Santos, *Azulejaria em Portugal nos séculos XV e XVI: introdução geral*, Lisboa, Fundação Calouste Gulbenkian, 1990.

[163] Cf. GUSMÃO, Adriano de, *O Nuno Gonçalves da Phaidon: Erros, omissões e plágios,* Lisboa, Europa-América, [s.d.].

[164] Cf. SMITH, Robert, *The art of Portugal, 1500-1800*, London, Weindenfeld and Nicolson, 1968.

[165] Cf. KUBLER, George Alexander, *A forma do tempo: observações sobre a história dos objectos*, Lisboa, Vega, 1991.

[166] Cf. GUSMÃO, Artur Nobre de, *Românico português do noroeste: alguns motivos geométricos na escultura decorativa*, Lisboa, Vega, 1992.

[167] Cf. FRANÇA, José Augusto, *A arte em Portugal no século XIX*, Lisboa, Bertrand, 1981.

[168] Cf. OLEIRO, João Manuel Bairrão, *Novos elementos para a história de "aeminium"*, Coimbra, Coimbra Editora, 1952.

[169] Cf. SILVA, Jorge Henrique Pais da, *Páginas de História da Arte*, Lisboa, Estampa, 1986.

[170] Cf. GONÇALVES, Flávio, *História da arte: iconografia e crítica*, Lisboa, Imprensa Nacional Casa da Moeda, 1990.

[171] Cf. MARKL, Dagoberto, *O essencial sobre Nuno Gonçalves*, Lisboa, Imprensa Nacional Casa da Moeda, 1987.

)[173], José Fernandes Pereira (1953-2012)[174], Paulo Varela Gomes (1952-)[175], Paulo Pereira (1957-)[176], Margarida Calado (1947-)[177] and Raquel Henriques da Silva (1952-)[178].

---

[172] *Cf.* MOREIRA, Rafael, *A arquitectura militar do Renascimento em Portugal*, Coimbra, Epatur, 1981.

[173] *Cf.* SERRÃO, Vítor, *A Pintura Maneirista em Portugal*, Lisboa, Instituto de Cultura e Lingua Portuguesa, 1991.

[174] *Cf.* PEREIRA, José Fernandes, *A Cultura Artística Portuguesa, Sistema Clássico*, Lisboa, [s.n.], 1999.

[175] *Cf.* GOMES, Paulo Varela, *A Confissão de Cyrillo: Estudos de História da Arte e da Aquitectura*, Lisboa Hiena, 1992.

[176] *Cf.* PEREIRA, Paulo, *História da Arte Portuguesa*, 3 Volumes, Lisboa, Círculo de Leitores, 1995.

[177] *Cf.* SILVA, Jorge Henrique Pais da & CALADO, Margarida, *Dicionário de termos de arte e arquitectura*, Barcarena, Editorial Presença, 2005.

[178] *Cf.* SILVA, Raquel Henriques da, *Aurélia de Souza*, Lisboa, Inapa, 1992.

Aesthetic methodologies themes

Scientific and philosophical knowledge must be based on curiosity and amazement, seeking new facts, problem solving or new ideas. With this, making known what was unknown was open, unproven phenomena or metaphysical explanations[179].

The scientific and philosophical explanation serves to rave less.

The scientific spirit was born in Ancient Greece, at the time of Socrates (468-399 BC), Plato (427-347 BC?) And Aristotle (384-322 BC) and before these, the Pre-Socratics who tried to explain what the ultimate substance of cosmos (metaphysical explanation)[180].

Man seeks to know how human beings came about and what their end is. For Kant, the question of "what is man?" Was crucial and all the big questions end up in this[181].

---

[179] POPPER, Karl, 'Conhecimento Objectivo e Subjectivo', in *O Conhecimento e o Problema Corpo-Mente*, Lisboa, Edições 70, pp. 13- 43.

[180] DAVIES, Henry H., 'Origen's Theory of Knowledge', in *The American Journal of Theology*, Volume 2, Number 4, 1898, pp. 737-762.

MOURELATOS, Alexander P., 'Pre-Socratic Origins of the Principle that There are No Origins from Nothing', in *The Journal of Philosophy*, Volume 78, Number 11, 1981, pp. 649-665.

HEIDEL, William Arthur, 'ΠερὶΦύσεως. A Study of the Conception of Nature among the Pre-Socratics', in *Proceedings of the American Academy of Arts and Sciences*, Volume 45, Number 4, 1910, pp. 79-133.

[181] *Cf.* KANT, Immanuel, *Crítica da Razão Pura*, Lisboa, Fundação Calouste Gulbenkian, 1994.

MACKINNON, Edward, 'The Development of Kant's Conception of Scientific Explanation', in *Proceedings of the Biennal Meeting of the Philosophy of Science Association*, Volume 1, 1978, pp. 18-30.

In the Middle Ages, the center became theology and individually - the mystic[182]. With Galileo Galilei (1564-1642)[183] and modern science, which sought to explain natural phenomena, no longer focused on purpose, but on the meaning of things - how things work[184].

The old metaphysical questions reappear with German philosophers: why being and not nothing. Immanuel Kant (1724-1804) summarized the fundamental questions and in the 20th century, with Martin Heidegger (1889-1976), the questions of Being (*Dasein*) are explored and that Georg Friedrich Hegel (1770-1831) and will call *Geist*[185].

Regarding ramblings, questions related to psychology were explained. It was also mentioned that someone only, since he did the psychoanalytic course (Sigmund Freud (1856-1939)[186] or Jacques Lacan (1901-1981)[187]), even if it is an illiterate of matter [188]. On the other hand, psychoanalytic questions have been reduced to the question that is listed as the

[182] OZMENT, Steven E., '"Homo Viator": Luther and Late Medieval Theology', in *The Harvard Theological Review*, Volume 62, Number 3, 1969, pp. 275-287.

MCGINN, Bernard, 'The Changing Shape of Late Medieval Mysticism', in *Church History*, Volume 65, Number 2, 1996, pp. 197-219.

[183] *Cf.* GALILEI, Galileu, *Sidereus Nuncius: O mensageiro das estrelas*, Lisboa, Fundação Calouste Gulbenkian, 2010.

[184] FINOCCHIARO, Maurice A., 'Galileo and the Philosophy of Science', in *PSA: Proceedings of the Biennal Meeting of the Philosophy of Science Association*, Volume 1, 1976, pp. 130-139.

ANDRADE, E.N., 'Galileo', in *Notes and Records of the Royal Society of London*, Volume 19, Number 2, 1964, pp. 120-130.

[185] HINCHMAN, Lewis P., 'The Origins of Human Rights: A Hegelian Perspective', in *The Western Political Quarterly*, Volume 37, Number 1, 1984, pp. 7-31.

[186] *Cf.* FREUD, Sigmund, *Essais de psychanalyse*, Paris, Payot, 1979.

[187] *Cf.* LACAN, *op. cit.*, 1995.

[188] HANSEN, Miriam Bratu, 'Benjamin's Aura', in *Critical Inquiry*, Volume 34, Number 2, 2008, pp. 336-375.

only one in the psychoanalytic search: am I a man or a woman?[189]

In the case of Art Science, it is cognitive, mathematical and objective, falling within a paradigm with a specific research method. This investigation is based on beliefs, techniques, values and models accepted by the community.

In the area of Social Sciences and Humanities, this consists of a positivist research paradigm that emerged in the 19th century, being more qualitative, empirical, interpretive, sociocritical, etc.[190]

The investigation consists of 6 steps: 1) Identify the problem; 2) State of the Art; 3) Specify the research purpose, methodology and working hypothesis; 4) Data collection; 5) Analysis and interpretation of data; and 6) Communication of results, conclusion and recommendation for future research. In the case of research in the arts, even an exhibition can be the subject of a doctoral thesis.

Aesthetics corresponds to "perception of the senses" in Greek and is linked to the idea of feeling with perception and not with the heart. Several examples of words that arose from the Greek word "aesthetics" were also counted.

Aesthetic issues are addressed in Plato in the works *Íon*[191], *Hípias Maior*[192], *Fedro*[193], *O Banquete*[194] and Book X of *República*[195].

---

[189] PARTNER, Nancy F., 'No Sex, No Gender', in *Speculum*, Volume 68, Number 2, 1993, pp. 419-443.

[190] SPIEGEL, Gabrielle M., 'Revising the Past / Revisiting the Present: How Change Happens in Historiography', in *History and Theory*, Volume 46, Number 4, 2007, pp. 1-19.

[191] *Cf.* PLATÃO, *Íon*, Lisboa, Inquérito, 2000.

[192] *Cf.* PLATÃO, *Hípias Maior*, Coimbra, Instituto Nacional de Investigação Científica, 1985.

In Aristotle (384-322 B.C.), these issues are addressed in the work *Poética*[196], in which aesthetic issues were part of a branch of philosophy and it was only with Alexander Baumgarten (1714-1764) in 1750 that it became an autonomous discipline[197].

Still in Kant and Hegel, aesthetics are reflected as a chapter in philosophy[198]. Kant, at the time of the Copernican revolution in philosophy, clarifies the Beautiful as a subjective condition, whose faculties are responsible for what we feel about our own things, that is, the effect that the object has under our faculties (*free game*)[199].

PENEDA, João Manuel, *O que é o belo?: comentário ao diálogo Hípias Maior*, trabalho de síntese, Lisboa, Faculdade de Belas-Artes da Universidade de Lisboa, 1997.

[193] *Cf.* PLATÃO, *Fedro*, Lisboa, Edições 70, 1997.

[194] *Cf.* PLATÃO, *O Banquete,* Lisboa, Edições 70, 1991.

[195] *Cf.* PLATÃO, *A república*, Livro X, Lisboa, Fundação Calouste Gulbenkian, 1983.

[196] *Cf.* ARISTÓTELES, *Poética*, Lisboa, Fundação Calouste Gulbenkian, 2004.

[197] *Cf.* BAUMGARTEN, Alexander, *Esthétique: précédée des Méditations philosophiques sur quelques sujets se rapportant à l'essence du poèm et de la métaphysique*, Paris, L'Herne, 1988.

WESSELL, Leonard P., 'Alexander Baumgarten's Contribution to the Development of Aesthetics', in *The Journal of Aesthetics and Art Criticism*, Volume 30, Number 3, 1972, pp. 333-342.

[198] *Cf.* KANT, Immanuel, *Crítica da Faculdade do Juízo*, Lisboa, Imprensa Nacional Casa da Moeda, 1992.

HEGEL, Friedrich, *Estética*, Lisboa, Guimarães Editores, 1993.

PENEDA, João Manuel, *A formulação kantiana da problematicidade estética*, Provas de aptidão pedagógica e capacidade científica, Faculdade de Belas-Artes da Universidade de Lisboa, 1997.

[199] GUYER, Paul, 'Free Play and True Well-Being: Herder's Critique of Kant's Aesthetics', in *The Journal of Aesthetics and Art Criticism*, Volume 65, Number 4, 2007, pp. 353-368.

Aesthetics for Hermann Lotze (1817-1881) begins in the psychological circumstance of mismatch (impressions / sensations) and is reflected as a linguistic difference based on the Platonic theory that distinguishes Beautiful and Pleasant[200].

Aesthetics at the Faculty of Fine Arts is not limited to aesthetic facts, but by the history of theoretical conception where the current formulation is: what conditions our aesthetic experience?

Aesthetic research methods are divided into four major groups: creation, work, appreciation and art in general / concepts / history. As long as the question "what is life?" Remains open, so will the question of "what is art?"[201].

Within the research in Aesthetics we can enumerate several aspects / paths to follow: philosophical, metaphysical, mystical, theological, initially, transcendental, hermeneutic, phenomenological, introspective, psychological, psychoanalytic, historical, sociological, linguistic, formal, semiotic, analytical, pragmatic research, anthropological, cultural, deconstructive, empirical, experimental, biological or neurological, etc.

In short, the object of aesthetics is very comprehensive, it is an aesthetic record in the maximum expression in art. On the

WICKS, Robert, 'Kant on Fine Art: Artistic Sublimity Shaped by Beauty', in *The Journal of Aesthetics and Art Criticism*, Volume 53, Number 2, 1995, pp. 189-193.

BURGESS, Craig, 'Kant's Key to the Critique of Taste', in *The Philosophical Quarterly*, Volume 39, Number 157, 1989, pp. 484-192.

[200] LOTZE, Hermann, *Outlines of Aesthetics*, trans. e ed. por G. Ladd, Boston, 1885, p. 20.

RAMPLEY, Matthew, 'From Symbol to Allegory: Aby Warburg's Theory of Art', in *The Art Bulletin*, Volume 79, Number 1, 1997, pp. 41-55.

[201] MOLNAR, F., 'Experimental Aesthetics or the Science of Art', in *Leonardo*, Volume 7, Number 1, 1974, pp. 23-26.

MUNRO, Thomas, 'Knowledge and Control in the Field of Aesthetics', in *The Journal of Aesthetics and Art Criticism*, Volume 1, Number 1, 1941, p. 1-12.

other hand, for many theorists, aesthetics deals with artistic creation. The research examples given in this session were based on works from the history of aesthetics that can be summarized in the bibliography presented by Raymond Bayer[202].

---

[202] *Cf.* BAYER, Raymond, *História da Estética*, Lisboa, Estampa, 1995.

Artistic anatomy: mime

The frieze of the condemned in the eardrum of the Cathedral of Saint-Lazare of Autun shows the sadness through the expression of the body.

On the contrary, a drawing with few strokes can convey joy, as in the case of a smile, or even with the textual application of "=)"[203]. This mimic of the body, as can be demonstrated by the expression of euphoria in the registered image of Cristiano Ronaldo, also expressed by the opening of the upper limbs.

The alteration of the natural orifices of the face is carried out through muscles. This is an organ formed by muscle cells and the order is given through a motor nerve. If in a muscle made up of 100 cells, only 10% are contracted, there may be no movement, but it gives the muscle tone.

The jaw bone is the only movable bone in the head, performs lowering and voice-over and is where some of the muscles responsible for mimicry (temples) will be fixed.

When the chewing muscles contract (temporal, masseter and pterygoid), the mandible rises to the jaw. However, the rest of the time, part of the cells are contracted and the mouth is closed. Otherwise, we would walk with our mouths open due to gravity[204]. Still on the mimicry of the face and as a curiosity, the skeleton being the base, the bony part does not include the nose because it consists of cartilage.

---

[203] DRESNER, Eli & HERRING, Susan C., 'Functions of the Non-Verbal in CMC: Emotions and Illocutionary Force, in *Communication Theory*, in press, University of Indiana, Available at http://info.ils.indiana.edu/~herring/emoticons.pdf [12-01-2015].

[204] See more at http://www.phys.nthu.edu.tw/classnews/96intr_phys/0706_Gravity%20 Theory.pdf [12-01-2015].

On the other hand, when we sleep, the cells fall asleep and decrease in number, and in this way, we open the mouth and even if it is not apparent, part of the cells remain contracted[205].

In the mimic of sadness, as the muscles are not contracted by gravity, the shoulders fall and the head is lowered, the natural orifices of the face will open, the orbicularis muscles of the eyes contract, semicircle and the corners of the mouth closed down and out[206]. The gravitational center of the head passes slightly in front of the first cervical vertebrae that supports it with anteflexion of the head[207].

In the mimic of sadness, there is a supraciliary muscle that contracts upward and outward and causes the outer 2/3 of the supracilia to move downward and inward, forming two oblique lines, eyes slightly closed, the folds of the eyes sagging, the eyelid cleft does not make a horizontal line, but with an oblique downward[208]. On the other hand, the corners of the mouth out and down and the chin muscle, the pout, which pulls the lower lip outward, with lowering of the natural orifices[209].

The functioning of the body is based on the action of the muscles and their contraction. Contrary to the previous mimicry, in the case of laughter what happens are the corners of the mouth pulled, the mouth turned upwards and the teeth are displayed, and if it is wider, you can see the teeth of the jaw[210].

---

[205] Definition of 'Sleep', Available at http://www.neuroanatomy.wisc.edu/coursebook/neuro10(2).pdf [12-01-2015].

[206] BARASCH, Moshe, 'The Crying Face', in *Artibus et Historiae*, Volume 8, Number 15, 1987, pp. 21-36.
ROUVIÉRE, H., *Anatomie Humaine: Descriptive, topographique et fonctionnelle*, Volume 1, 1948, p. 164.

[207] Idem, p. 166.

[208] ROUVIÉRE, *op. cit.*, pp. 162/163

[209] Ibidem.

[210] ROUVIÉRE, *op. cit.*, p. 162.

The eyes, on the other hand, slightly squint with the orbicularis contracting, with the appearance of laugh lines and frank laughter, these diverge in the corner in the form of a small fan.

As a mirror of the soul, the eyes are the ones that give more mimic indication[211]. In fact, through the analysis of the eyes it is possible to identify a large number of emotions, the eyes and eyebrows being very important for mimicry and their respective identification[212].

In the case of other primates, there is a social smile, according to the decisions of the tribe[213]. On the other hand, we can give the inter-species example of dogs and their affection

---

[211] *Where Aristotle had emphasized the structure of the face, Cicero emphasized its expressiveness: 'everything is in the face, and the face in turn is totally dominated by the eyes... the face is the mirror of the soul... for this is the only part of the body capable of displaying as many expressions as there are emotions'.* SYNNOTT, Anthony, 'Truth and Goodness, Mirrors and Masks – Part I: A Sociology of Beauty and the Face', in *The British Journal of Sociology*, Volume 40, Number 4, 1989, pp. 607-636.

See more at SYNNOTT, Anthony, 'Truth and Goodness, Mirrors and Masks Part II: A Sociology of Beauty and the Face', in *The British Journal of Sociology,* Volume 41, Number 1, 1990, pp. 55-76.

[212] GROSSMAN, Ruth B. & TAGER-FLUSBERG, Helen, 'Reading faces for information about words and emotions in adolescents with autism', in *Research in Autism Spectrum Disorders*, Volume 2, 2008, pp. 681-695.

ADOLPHS, Ralph, *Recognizing Emotion From Facial Expressions: Psychological and Neurological Mechanisms*, University of Iowa College of Medicine, 2002. Available at http://emotion.caltech.edu/papers/Adolphs2002Recognizing.pdf [12-01-2015].

CALVO, Manuel G. & FERNÁNDEZ-MARTÍN, Andrés, 'Can the eyes reveal a person's emotions? Biasing role of the mouth expression', in *Motivation and Emotion*, DOI 10.1007/s11031-012-9298-1.

[213] SCHREIBER, Darren, 'Political Cognition as Social Cognition: Are We All Political Sophisticates?', Abstract submitted to *The Political Dynamics of Thinking and Feeling,* October 18, 2004. Available at http://www.uiowa.edu/~c030111/decisionmaking/grad2005/schreiber2.pdf [25-01-2015].

developed with humans thousands of years ago, creating relationships based on intuition and rational association of actions[214].

There are cultures where there is no fear of mimic expressiveness, allowing the mimicry of the body to express itself. However, there are other extremes, such as Japan, where children are educated not to let their face transmit feelings and emotions, interpreted as an invasion of privacy[215]. It's a social smile, it doesn't correspond to emotion, *that Japanese smile so difficult to understand*[216].

The Portuguese creation of the "yellow smile" to designate the eastern peoples who were designated as yellow, stems from when the Portuguese arrived at their lands and were received with such an expression. The yellow smile muscle is very weak and asymmetrical, and this smile is very common - one of the corners is more pulled. The "risorius" muscle is the main driver of this action.

As an example and both enigmatic, the Kouroi exhibited the half smile in Ancient Greece, as well as the smile of La Gioconda in the early 16th century.

In the smile, the zygomatic muscles contract, pulling the corners of the mouth out and up, and the "risorius" pulls the corners back. In joy, the nose muscles also contract, dilating the nostrils, which accompany the smile. In the case of the actors,

---

[214] RAILTON, Peter, 'The Affective Dog and Its Rational Tale: Intuition and Attunement', in *Ethics*, Volume 124, Number 4, 2014, pp. 813-859.

[215] ROYCE, Josiah, 'Race Questions and Prejudice', in *International Journal of Ethics*, Volume 16, Number 3, 1906, pp. 265-288.

Iwasaki, Noriko, 'Learning L2 Japanese "Politeness" and "Impoliteness": Young American Men's Dilemmas during Study Abroad', in *Japanese Language and Literature*, Volume 45, Number 1, 2011, pp. 67-106.

[216] GUILLAIN, R., 'Japanese Uncertainties', in *International Affairs*, Volume 26, Number 3, 1950, pp. 329-338.

they have a dual role - to disguise real feelings and represent those of the script.

We can also give three more examples, such as the mimic of attention, of those who meditate, and in a way, close in on themselves, slightly narrowing their eyes and the natural holes in the face are normal[217]. On the other hand, in the expression of cholera, we will have enlarged nostrils, wrinkles between the eyes by contraction of the pyramidal muscle, mouth may be contracted and closed and the eyebrows are down, forming wrinkles by contraction of the supraciliary[218]. Finally, in the mimic of admiration, the eyes are opened to the maximum, with the horizontal forehead wrinkles formed by contraction of the frontal and supraciliary muscles.

Mimicry is important in the representation of human beings and is often used as mimicry in the humanized animation of animal figures.

One of the Marketing applications is the use of design to convey a message, such as the number of teeth, that is, gradation of smile intensity that can be important, where the reference "a smile with 4 teeth or 6 teeth" is used .

In some cultures, women shaved their eyebrows and painted over them because it was easier to disguise emotions. In Francisco de Holanda, in Tirar pelo natural (original edition of 1549), he mentions some "goofs" who shaved their eyebrows to hide their natural expression[219].

By nature, the face and posture express natural human emotions[220], instead of the verbal language that allows to hide

---

[217] ROUVIÉRE, op. cit., p. 165.

[218] Idem, pp. 163-166.

[219] HOLANDA, Francisco de, Do tirar pelo natural, Lisboa, Livros Horizonte, 1984, pp. 27/28.

[220] WIERZBUCKA, Anna, 'Human Emotions: Universal or Cultural-Specific?', in American Anthropologist, Volume 88, Number 3, 1986, pp. 584-594.

feelings. A very important role in mime is that of the human hand, in addition to its manipulative function. However, opposing the mimic of acceptance, that of refusal, is reflected in the extension of the fingers, forearm and arm, making a movement away[221].

In fact, what distinguishes us from "non-human primate" mammals is the possibility of being able to oppose the pulp of the thumb to the other fingers[222].

On the other hand, still on mime, politicians make gestures as if they are fixing, transmitting the idea of organization and coherence[223].

Mirror neurons, when observed, we will respond by similarity[224], yawning being the most common[225].

Marco Aurélio says "Your speech was written on your forehead: I read it before you spoke", in his famous work *Meditations*[226]. In fact, the study of physiognomy has been extensively deepened, with a natural emphasis on the work of Artur Ramos[227], but the area of knowledge studied since AD II[228].

ALANEN, Lilli, 'What Are Emotions about?', in *Philosophy and Phenomenological Research*, Volume 67, Number 2, 2003, pp. 311-334.

[221] O mesmo que "recolhe".

[222] Formando uma pinça natural.

[223] KENDON, Adam, 'Gesture', in *Annual Review of Anthropology*, Volume 26, 1997, pp. 109-128.

[224] COOK, Richard, BIRD, Geoffrey, CATMUR, Caroline, PRESS, Clare & HEYES, Cecilia, 'Mirror neurons: From origin to function', in *The Behavioral and Brain Sciences*, Volume 37, 2014, pp. 177-241.

[225] HAKER, Helene, KAWOHL, Wolfram, HERWIG, Uwe & ROSSIER, Wulf, 'Mirror neuron activity during contagious yawning-an fMRI study', in *Brain Imaging and Behaviour*, Volume 7, Issue 1, pp. 28-34.

[226] BRUNT, P. A., 'Marcus Aurelius in His Meditations', in *The Journal of Roman Studies*, Volume 64, 1974, pp. 1-20

[227] RAMOS, Artur, *Retrato: o desenho da Presença*, Lisboa, Campo da Comunicação, 2010.

In other animals, we did not get this type of identifying elements already covered, but there are other signs that allow us to identify emotions, a great example of which is the ears and the tail.

In animals it goes through other elements, and in humans it will be to communicate with the group.

Mimicry was discovered by direct stimulation by electrodes in a patient in the 18th century, who lost sensitivity but not the ability to contract facial muscles[229].

In Egypt, the canon was represented in Egyptians, but not foreigners, with feet represented by the inner view and the narrowest rib line.

Palm, forearm and biceps muscle are related and positioned in a way that makes no sense. Even so, in the female case, they had fat mark on the belly that is characteristic of the female sex, with a marked pubic triangle, accentuating the width of the hips.

The theme of human representation has always been around the human body and even in Naturalism, the human body has always escaped the rules of the classic canon (canon of Policleto)[230].

Anatomy was little applied objectively in the area of artistic production, having always been idealized to what is real and, in the end, being the objective of art, to allow the interpretation of things and objects in another way.

---

[228] EVANS, Elizabeth C., 'The Study of Physiognomy in the Second Century A.D.', in *Transactions and Proceedings of the American Philolofical Association*, Volume 72, 1941, pp. 96-108.

[229] BLANC, Yves & DIMANICO, Ugo, 'History of the Study of Skeletal Muscle Function with Emphasis on Kinesiological Electromyography', in *The Open Rehabilitation Journal*, Volume 3, 2010, pp. 84-93.

[230] TOBIN, Richard, 'The Canon of Polykleitos', in *American Journal of Archaeology*, Volume 79, Number 4, 1975, pp. 307-321.

Brighenti, Amorim and Conefrev

Paulo Brighenti (1968-), Manuel Amorim (1950-) and Alexandre Conefrey (1961-). The works of these artists are of drawing and have outstanding works, from three different generations. These three artists behave as a common subject in their creative process.

The first speaker, Paulo Brighenti, started by mentioning that his career began in the 90s and the work presented in this first part of the round table was based on a work in progress project by this artist, consisting mainly of large scale works and models made in studio.

Some of these works consist of mountains that were once volcanoes, always creating relationships between painting and drawing. The exhibition space allows to increase the scale used in the studio, and in the case of one of the particular works that was shown, it hid a vanitas. The space and perspective is worked in a contemplative sense.

In the technical execution process, the risk is intrinsically associated because it is something not designed, the method is changed to something spontaneous in its entirety, with hidden anamorphosis. This large-scale drawing "eats" the risk because it does not fade, painted directly on the wall, without concern for conservatives because it "lives by itself". It is done on the wall to show that it is a different domain and the issue of time directly related to the installation perspective[231].

In the extended drawing with abstraction, other drawings of lower dimensions with two drawings per sheet, give us the idea of a book. This one is drawn with lyrics from the song "Sara".

---

[231] Cf. AA.VV., *Os últimos dias: desenhos de Alexandre Conefrey, Paulo Brighenti, Rui Moreira, Rui Vasconcelos*, Lisboa, Centro de Arte Moderna José De Azeredo Perdigão, 2000.

The drawing saves and the painting fails, because it is read through its impossibility.

The painting is always the same, he is always trying to do it. - Quote by Paulo Brighenti in this communication.

Relationship drawing on the wall with bench with models on top, transposing the notion of scale. Modeling of the skull with a ghostly side of mirror duplicity, with dimensions of 1.20 m by 1.50 m, with dry pastel water.

Other installations that cover walls with yellow pigment and paper models, with crushed dry pastel and rubbed on the wall.

The second speaker at this roundtable, Manuel Amorim, held an exhibition of works carried out between 2002 and 2010, beginning the "HEARTS" series, where he explores dimensions of color, atmosphere and light[232].

The purpose of these drawings was, within the same work of representing the human figure (silhouette), to try to find something within these silhouettes. This organic minimalism is centered only on a figure and which escapes the geometric, is organic and reduced to an essence, with dimensions between 50 and 70 cm.

Something that can be represented, not a heart, but the metaphor of the heart, as if the body were torn, looking for plastic solutions that would allow this opening, through various dimensions.

In this case, drawing is support for painting and not a purpose. At a certain point it is no longer a heart, it is a metaphor, with various supports and materials, graphite, charcoal, china ink, oil, etc., creating countless variations on the same theme.

---

[232] Consult more works on the author's ®Facebook. Available at https://www.facebook.com/manuel.amorim.169/photos_all [12-01-2015].

The metaphor gap is always different, and it becomes an abstraction, and it can be anything you want, creating an enigma. Because these figures are with enigmatic or uncertain postures like Beckett characters[233].

As a varied support, even plain paper, each one brings its own solution, its performance, and in this artist in particular, there is a creative process developed using the watercolor technique.

In the "HAMON3" series, with 2 by 1.5 m screens, the pigments are applied raw, mixed with resin. In this series, the positions are fluid as if they were nerves or blood circulatory schemes, represented through the expressive plasticity that these materials allow. Curiously, this artist prepares all his materials, from the canvas, the preparation layer with plaster and sand as if it were an epidermis, without any protection.

On the other hand, he confesses to having exhausted the theme itself, being the color parameter of enormous relevance, but always with creative and never decorative objectivity. For this artist, direct work with the pigments prepared by himself allows for expansion at the procedural level, but it is not feasible for working with large dimensions.

The chosen theme is to explore the human figure in a close-up view, in relation to the cinema in question and the approach of a medium plane (zoom in).

Still in material and conservative terms, it is interesting that this author uses good quality grids and applies wedges that allow greater stability after material application and drying of materials. On the other hand, Manuel Amorim keeps a record of all his works, creating a database, where he keeps (whenever possible) the whereabouts of his works.

---

[233] WECHSLER, Judith, 'Illustrating Samuel Beckett: The Issue of the Supererogatory', in *Art Journal*, Volume 52, Number 4, 1993, pp. 33-40.

The last speaker at this round table, Alexandre Conefrey, presented works related to the theme of freedom, which, as an artist and how he deals with the production of the few times he lives. That is, it explores the dimensions of production and alteration of registration and the way they are seen by others. How do we deal with art and what are the limits as an artist? - Quote by Alexandre Conefrey in this communication.

This artist started by presenting watercolors from the year 2000, related to military scenes, battle tactics, flowers and leaves that he described or transposed onto paper[234].

On the other hand, he made plastic explorations related to the theme of 9/11. For this artist, his works represent narratives, but they are not narratives in themselves. As if telling a story, but not having a story to tell, but as we transpose it, which is not directly noticeable, it only presents itself as aesthetics that is within a story.

In a second phase, it presented production in which it uses the use of Japanese paper to create purposeful cracks. In this case, the best materials allow greater fulfillment of the purpose of the work for aesthetic and plastic enjoyment. In this case, it is in the failures that the solutions for perception are found.

There is a creative process through the design of small notebooks where the idea is placed up to larger scales and final work.

Finally, the series "Mockingbird", with a bird that imitates the voice of other birds, using materials such as graphite and colored pencils, produced when listening to Bach's songs. Hence the idea of singing to imitate anything, leading to the reflection of

---

[234] *Cf.* AA.VV., *op. cit.*, 2000.

"us" artists and how we "see" art, art after Marcel Duchamp (1887-1968)[235].

In this work there is a connection with the artist when interpreting the music, whose vertical lines with dots directed in black gray and blue, allow extrapolating to a mutation and freedom in which we "believe" in what "we" are doing regardless of how it is motivated or the materials used.

At the end of the session, there was space for a small debate on "what it is like to be an artist", having all unanimously answered that it is very difficult to be only an artist, but it is not worth giving up for something that is done with passion, how is art.

---

[235] Cf. DUVE, Thierry de, *Kant after Duchamp*, Cambridge, The MIT Press, 1996.

Image and photography

These are constituted as geometric operations, not only dominant vanishing points of the spatial directions and spatial planes, but also the location of implicit geometric elements related to the linear conical perspective

In this way, it is possible to analyze geometric elements present in the images, such as markings, constructions and corrections that allow detecting the veracity or falsity of the strokes. On the other hand, these perceptual restitutions also make it possible to obtain calculations of the geometric elements implicit in the images and, in conjunction with other known reference elements, to reconstruct real-scale dimensions of spaces.

In this way, the combination of these elements allows to know or complete parts of fragments initially unknown.

This process is based on the collection of essential data, these being the main points of escape and distance. It is worth safeguarding the hypothesis that these surveys lead us to discover possible cases of perceptual inaccuracies.

In the case of photography, the interest in applying this technique makes it possible to prospectively restore the image in question and, eventually, move from the central conical system to the double orthogonal projection system, restoring plans and elevations, based on the knowledge of the viewing distance, height of vision and other elements.

From the extensive procedure described in this session, it is worth highlighting only the objective and potential of this technique, leaving the example of the perspective restitution from a photograph[236].

On the other hand, the return of an oblique frame was also addressed, based on the same technique as the previous one, but based on aerial vanishing points[237]. In this case, like the previous one, we started with the use of a camera and a record of the interior of the Basilica da Estrela in Lisbon.

An interesting topic for a PhD would be to apply this methodology in Baroque paintings (linear perspective) and to reconstitute spaces, taking into account the perspective knowledge of the time of its execution[238].

Some theses have already looked into the methods and techniques that artists are likely to use to create illusory painting on a vaulted ceiling[239].

---

[236] Consultable process at JANTZEN, Éric, *Traité Pratique de Perspective de photographie et de dessin appliqués à l'architecture et au paysagei,* Paris, La Villette Eds De, 1996, p. 144-155.

[237] BARTRINA, Luís Villanueva, *Perspectiva lineal, Su Construcción y su Relación con la Fotografia*, Barcelona, Edicions UPC, 1996, pp. 152-169.

[238] TRINDADE, António de Oriol, 'A recepção do modelo de perspectiva linear renascentista a norte e a oeste dos Alpes e um exemplo concreto no Museu Nacional de Arte Antiga em Lisboa', in *Arte Teoria*, Número 6, 2005, pp. 51-73.

Idem, 'A perspectiva linear na pintura: a família do Visconde de Santarém, de Domingos António Sequeira', in *Arte Teoria*, Número 12/13, 2010, pp. 133-138.

See example of its application in the work of Piero della Francesca em ELKINS, James, 'Piero della Francesca and the Renaissance Proof of Linear Perspective', in *Art Bulletin*, Volume 69, Number 2, 1987, pp. 220-230.

[239] *Cf.* SANTOS, Pedro, *O Trompe L'Oeil Barroco na Igreja do Menino Deus em Lisboa: métodos e técnicas*, Tese de Doutoramento em Belas Artes, especialidade em Geometria, Faculdade de Belas-Artes da Universidade de Lisboa, Lisboa, 2014.

On the other hand, we also have the example in vaulted ceilings of churches in Lisbon, where artists used insightful methods and techniques to create illusory paintings on the vaulted ceiling[240].

In fact, there are countless perspective treaties that we know[241], it is worth noting yet the use of the obscure camera by Johannes Vermeer (1635-1675), resulting in paintings with a perfect perspective[242].

Finally, the interesting hypothesis of applying this method and technique to the paintings of Edward Hopper (1882-1967) was put forward, and in fact, having achieved the state of the art, it was possible to assess the beginning of studies in this direction[243].

REIS, Vítor dos, *O Rapto do Observador: Invenção, Representação e Percepção do Espaço Celestial na Pintura de Tectos em Portugal no Século XVIII*, Tese de doutoramento em Belas Artes, especialidade em Cultura e Forma Visual, Faculdade de Belas-Artes da Universidade de Lisboa, Lisboa, 2006.

[240] Cf. TRINDADE, António, *Um Olhar Sobre a Perspectiva Linear Em Portugal, Nas Pinturas De Cavalete, Tectos e Abóbadas: 1470-1816*, Tese de doutoramento em Belas Artes, especialidade em Geometria Descritiva, Faculdade de Belas-Artes da Universidade de Lisboa, Lisboa, 2008.

REIS, *op. cit.*, 2006.

SANTOS, Pedro, *op. cit.*, 2014.

[241] Cf. VELTMAN, Kim H., 'Literature on Perspective: A Select Bibliography (1971-1984)', In *Marburger Jahrbuch für Kinstwissenschaft*, Volume 21, 1986, pp. 185-207.

[242] MILLS, Allan A., 'Vermeer and the Camera Obscura: Some Practical Considerations', in *Leonardo*, Volume 31, Number 3, 1998, pp. 213-218.

[243] GILLIES, Jean, 'Timeless Space of Edward Hopper', in *Art Journal*, Volume 31, Number 4, 1972, pp. 404-412.

Science at the service of art

The history of science, like the history of all human ideas, is a history of irresponsible dreams, of obstinacy, and of error. But science is one of the very few human activities — perhaps the only one — in which errors are systematically criticized and fairly often, in time, corrected. This is why we can say that, in science, we often learn from our mistakes, and why we can speak clearly and sensibly about making progress there. (POPPER, 2002, p. 293)

Throughout the nuclei of this first semester, topics related to the research methodology were addressed. On the one hand, more conventional methodologies in Fine Arts, or even more recent ones, such as museology and curatorship. However, none of the sessions covered a methodology that would include an inter-, trans- and multidisciplinary project.

On the other hand, other interesting interventions, such as teaching, not only from the Academy of Fine Arts, but also from the Free Design Schools, allow an approach to the state of the art regarding the doctoral project under development.

Finally, and of enormous relevance, the application of science in artistic objects and also, the session referring to the exhibition of the creative process of 3 Portuguese artists, as well as the session referring to Geometry applied to photography and painting. In fact, we have entered an area in which different fields of knowledge come together to obtain new knowledge.

The PhD project aims to study the creative process of painting nude model, or designated as an academic, from the 19th century, and based on this presentation that will address the theme in this report. This study of the process, in order to understand how Expressionism was absorbed in the Academy, requires the help of more conventional methodologies to art history, but essentially using science[244].

In fact, the state of the art regarding production within the academy has been vast[245], serving as a grounding guide to support the teaching method. On the other hand, production within this institution, already covered by both sessions by Margarida Calado and Eduardo Duarte within the scope of the Science of Art nucleus of November 7, 2014, summarized in this report[246].

However, all of these studies focus on works and documentation, with a visual and sometimes technical perspective, but based on documentation. In this way, the perspective of this project is obviously based on all the existing and essential documentation for justification and support for academic scientific conclusion, but it intends to focus essentially on materiality and technique in a profound way.

Much of the knowledge we have about the execution technique and the materials applied in the production of nude model painting at the Lisbon Academy is, unfortunately, oral[247].

However, more and more science has helped other areas such as art history and conservation and restoration[248]. In this

---

[244] See the excellent and recent work carried out by the Musée du Louvre team (Paris), application of multimedia in these areas of knowledge addressed here, Available at http://focus.louvre.fr/fr/la-joconde/comparer/les-examens-scientifiques [20-01-2014].

[245] CARDEIRA, Ana Mafalda, *Caracterização material e técnica de 12 pinturas de académia de nu de José Veloso Salgado, pertencentes à coleção da FBAUL*, Dissertação de Mestrado em Ciências da Conservação, Restauro e Produção de Arte Contemporânea, Faculdade de Belas-Artes da Universidade de Lisboa, Lisboa, 2014.

[247] On the other hand, it is possible to find some handwritten references in works published by Torre do Tombo, Available at http://digitarq.arquivos.pt/results?t=academia+belas+artes [29-01-2015].

institution, complementary knowledge begins to germinate the historical and artistic data already known[249].

Having already carried out a case study, resulting in a publication of an article of international circulation with scientific arbitration, on the painting of *A Família de Caim* (1891), by José Veloso Salgado (1864-1945), it is intended to demonstrate the usefulness of science in plastic arts and, in this case in concrete, in oil painting.

Veloso Salgado as a student of Fernand Cormon (1845-1924), executed the copy of *Caïn*, in 1891, of his master during his stay in Paris[250]. Confirming the idea that it is a copy of Cormon's original, currently on display at the Musée d'Orsay[251].

What is the interest of studying this work? Not only because it is a copy of a master like Fernand Cormon, but also because it was executed by Veloso Salgado as a State pensioner.

From the examination methods[252], it was possible to unveil a grid from which Veloso Salgado would have relied on to

---

[248] DELBOURGO, S., 'Sauver l'Art? Conserver: Analyser: Restaurer by François Schweizer: Anne Rinuy', in *Studies in Conservation*, Volume 28, Number 2, 1983, pp. 95-96.

[249] Or yet to know, citing Karl Popper, *Our knowledge can only be finite, while our ingnorance must necessarily be infinite.* POPPER, Karl, 'Knowledge without Authority (1960)', in *Theory of Knowledge: Selectrions*, MILLER, D. (Ed.), Princeton, Princeton University Press, 1985, pp. 46-57.

PANOFKSY, Erwin, 'On the Relationship of Art History and Art Theory: Towards the Possibility of a Fundamental System of Concepts for a Science of Art', in *Critical Inquiry*, Volume 35, Number 1, 2008, pp. 43-71.

[250] On this copy, see if the study developed by CARDEIRA et al., *Multi-analytical characterisation...*, pp. 271-274.

[251] Confirming the idea of a copy of the original *Caïn* (1880) by Fernand Cormon.

[252] Examination methods, analyzes performed resulting in images, such as photography, optical microscope image, radiography, etc., are designated, by CARDEIRA, *op. cit.*, 2014.

make a copy of Cormon's original work and areas of previous intervention (in white). In this way, taking into account the lack of information, it was possible to start a new chapter in the history of teaching, namely, the methodologies of execution used in the Academy of Fine Arts of Lisbon.

Obviously, the grid transposition method is much older than the period under study[253], but until today it had not been observed in other works copied from the same time, belonging to our collection and until now there was no information about the technique of this work[254].

This is to give an example of the possibilities of applying analytical science to art. However, it is necessary to be careful to turn to specialists, such as art historians, photographers, chemists, physicists, designers, etc., in order to maintain closer proximity to the truth.

4 stages of a possible research methodology to be used to carry out the master's project are now briefly announced, demonstrating the success of acquiring important results in the study of oil paintings[255].

STEP I. IN SITU SURVEY OF THE STATE OF PAINTINGS, WITH VISUAL REGISTRATION AND DOCUMENTAL COLLECTION

The survey of the state of conservation of the paintings allows to register their state, visual relations between represented figures and chromatic composition. The combination of documentation may contribute to an initial knowledge of the artistic and pedagogical level.

---

[253] WILLIAMSON, Jack H., 'The Grid: History, Use, and Meaning', in *Design Issues*, Volume 3, Number 2, 1986, pp. 15-30.

[254] CARDEIRA et al., *op. cit.*, pp. 271-274.

[255] *Cf.* CARDEIRA, *op. cit.*, 2014.

STEP II. SURFACE ANALYSES IN SITU DAS PAINTURAS

Photography under visible and grazing light allows you to observe details on the surface of the paintings from the resulting shadows, such as superficial cracking, waviness of the substrate, grid mark and scratches on the varnish.

Photography under transmitted light highlights gaps and differences in the thickness of the chromatic layers. The macro register allows details of intervention areas, cracks, tears, gaps, changes in the pictorial surface, pasting, brush marks, signature and stamps.

The set of these data allows a detailed record of the current state of conservation. Photography of fluorescence induced by ultraviolet radiation performed in situ is useful to obtain information on details of the surface of the paintings, such as fluorescence specific to each pigment, organic materials and varnishes of different times. It also allows to acquire information on the conservation status of the protection layer, to detect touch-up areas and to assist the conservative restorer in the cleaning process and consequent restoration treatment.

Infrared reflectography performed in situ has the added value of being non-invasive and non-destructive.

It allows to observe the existence or absence of drawing underlying the pictorial layers, areas of alteration or addition of later elements and to locate intervention areas at the level of the preparation layer. On the other hand, it also helps to locate points of analysis through X-ray fluorescence spectroscopy.

Optical microscopy in situ is performed using a digital microscope, equipped with visible and ultraviolet light. This technique allows to register in more detail zones for further analysis by means of X-ray fluorescence spectroscopy and later sampling for Raman and Fourier transform infrared spectroscopy.

The set of data acquired in this step represents an essential step for reflection on the execution technique, state of conservation and is essential to the next step.

STEP III. COMBINATION OF TECHNICAL CHARACTERIZATION FOR MATERIAL ANALYZES IN SITU AND ANALYTICAL TECHNIQUES FOR LABORATORY

X-ray fluorescence spectroscopy is performed in situ and has the added value of being noninvasive and non-destructive.

This technique allows the qualitative elementary analysis applied to the identification of elements present in the sample, allowing the simultaneous and rapid detection of several characteristic elements of a given inorganic pigment[256]. Together with the data acquired in the previous step, it allows the location of intervention and touch-up areas.

After collecting this first data, it is possible to choose the best sampling zones. This process will be carried out using needle tips suitable for micro sampling and carried out, whenever possible, in gap areas or painting edges. All micro-samples will be mounted in epoxy resin for analysis using Raman and Fourier transform infrared spectroscopy.

Raman spectroscopy, although non-destructive, requires sampling. Together with the results obtained by X-ray fluorescence spectroscopy, it allows to identify organic or inorganic compounds and to distinguish different crystalline structures in pigments with the same chemical formula. The coupling of microscopy to the Raman equipment allows analysis of micro samples. Fourier transform infrared spectroscopy allows to confirm specific pigments and to identify organic compounds[257]. This technique will also be used to identify

---

[256] Técnica abordada no **subcapítulo 2.1.1.**

[257] This analysis, although more complicated in terms of reading results, may help to understand a step in the technique of these painters. For example, the purity of the oil. That is, if in various FTIR analyzes of the

mediums in the same micro samples taken for Raman spectroscopy.

With this stage and the data from the previous one, all material and technical information is gathered.

STEP IV. CONFRONTATION OF ANALYTICAL DATA TO KNOW THE CREATIVE PROCESS AND METHODOLOGICAL SURVEY OF ARTISTIC TEACHING.

The confrontation of documentary sources and analytical data will allow us to understand the learning process arising from the academic tradition of fine arts. At this stage of the study, it will be possible to achieve the objective of knowing at a historical, aesthetic, pedagogical and methodological level the production of these nude academies and their relationship of 'absorption' in the face of national and international modernist influences. In this way, it will be possible to carry out a methodological survey of the artistic teaching process of the late

---

same painting, if there are no differences in the type of oil applied, the oil used by the painters would be the same or similar to the paint brand, or they would have ground the pigments and applied only one same oil for your application.

On the other hand, if there are different oils in the same painting, it indicates that in the technique it may be important to apply a certain oil for a certain effect - drying, chiaroscuro, fleshing - which can determine the final result, or even that the pigments they were already purchased in tubes (prepared), and the application of another oil would be for painting. Finally, it is known that casein was used in a first stage to apply the oil. This technique allows us to identify that compound and, in this way,, discern and draw conclusions about different methods of execution depending on its application or not. Bearing in mind that these paintings had a limited time of execution due to the time that the model was exposed, one would expect not to use this compound, however, it will be interesting to verify this assumption. Both positive and negative results will be extremely relevant for understanding the methodology.

19th century and the beginning of the following in the fine arts of Lisbon.

Finally, all this knowledge, its registration and treatment, will help conservation and restoration in future terms. It may be interesting to see why there are works in an advanced state of conservation compared to others, from the same period and kept in the same conditions.

Art and creativity

Nowadays, we try to absorb all the possible information, looking through the acquired experience, to know what Life is. Still, in structural terms, there is a hierarchy of questions that successively condition subsequent responses. Taking as an example the work of Immanuel Kant (1724-1804) and his attempt to systematize the search for these answers in the works of *A Crítica da Razão Pura*[258], *A Crítica da Razão Prática* and *A Crítica da Faculdade do Juízo*[259].

In fact, in each of these works, Kant seeks to respond with what we know, from ethics and morals (what should I do and how) to obtain answers at the level of the ends and ends of our existence. On the other hand, if there is a superior feeling, it is called Taste, defining what is "pleasant" (pleasure with quality), based only on sight and hearing, as Plato (427-347 BC?) Defends in your work *Hípias Maior*[260].

In this way, we can ask the following question: "Is there a pleasure with quality or not?". In other texts by Kant, namely on his considerations around metaphysics, we can find some reflection on what to expect after life. Still on this question, Kant summarizes all the questions to "what is man?", In which in anthropology from the transcendental point of view, being

---

[258] *Cf.* KANT, Immanuel – **Crítica da Razão Pura**. Lisboa: Fundação Calouste Gulbenkian, 1994.

[259] *Cf.* KANT, Immanuel – **Crítica da Faculdade do Juízo**. Lisboa: Imprensa Nacional Casa da Moeda, 1992.

[260] *Cf.* PLATÃO – **Hípias Maior**. Coimbra: Instituto Nacional de Investigação Científica, 1985.

PENEDA, João Manuel – **O que é o belo?: comentário ao diálogo Hípias Maior**. Trabalho de síntese. Lisboa: Faculdade de Belas-Artes da Universidade de Lisboa, 1997.

unable to answer philosophically, constituting as a proof the continuity of the existence of philosophy after Kant[261].

On the other hand, Martin Heidegger (1889-1976) also tried to answer the question "what is life?", With the designation "Dasein", continuing to search for these answers[262].

The word Art comes from the Latin Ars, meaning conduct or craft, and this noun depends on the use we give it, in which everything can be art (but not everything is art), depending on human ingenuity or even greater intelligence.[263]. The word *Techné*, mean artistic and aesthetic production[264].

In fact, art is the result of the freedom that the human has to change the world around him. On the other hand, the existence of art demonstrates that man has ceased to be an animal, using instruments that allowed him to carry out and develop artistic production.

Still, there is confusion between what art is and its origins, and on this issue, Adorno recalls that it is a mistake to embark on the essence of art as a starting point, in which man determines his own destiny[265]. Art opens up to man the lack of definition / unveiling of this essence as a departure, but it can fall by the

---

[261] *Cf.* FOUCAULT, Michael – **Introduction to Kant's Anthropology**. New York: Semiotext, 2008.

[262] *Cf.* HEIDEGGER, Martin – **Ser e tempo**. Petrólopis: Vozes, 1998.

HINCHMAN, Lewis P. – The Origins of Human Rights: A Hegelian Perspective. The Western Political Quarterly. pp. 7-31.

Cf. KANT, op. cit., 1994.

MACKINNON, Edward – The Development of Kant's Conception of Scientific Explanation. pp. 18-30.

[263] TETLOW, John – The Vocabulary of High-School Latin and How to Master It. pp. 18-29.

[264] SCHATZBERG, Eric – From Art to Applied Science. pp. 555-563.

[265] *Cf.* ADORNO, Theodor W. – **Teoria estética**. Lisboa: Edições 70, 1993.

wayside if it is not supported (in the case of "oral heritage" or immaterial).

In the case of "repression" in Kant, the symptom is linked to the repressed representation, ideas and words, being equivalent to the notion of "shadow" for Carl Gustav Jung (1875-1961)[266]. In fact, the issue of the repression of the sublime consists of the loss of fear, but also, and at the same time, of what is highest in us[267]. In this way, man tends, in some way, not to cover what is dark, but also what is most virtuous, removing obstacles and triggering what is higher. With this, it is possible to achieve the sublime, as something that is above the ground.

For Freud there was no philosophical speculation because he did not want to influence his clinical cases, despite being a frequent reader of Friedrich Nietzsche (1844-1900)[268]. The term "sublimation" is chosen by Nietzsche and later used by Sigmund Freud (1856-1939), in the latter art and science would be a positive case of sublimation[269].

On the other hand, for this last author, the improvement did not go through the impulse of the same, but through something external, namely the superego[270]. In other words, there is no internal impulse to sublimate ourselves as living

---

[266] WYNNE, Vincent W. – Abraham's Gift: A Psychoanalytical Christology. pp. 759-780.

KINGS, Steven – Jung's Hermeneutics of Scripture. pp. 233-251.

[267] PENEDA, João Manuel – Os paradoxos do sintoma e da sublimação: o contributo da teoria psicanalítica de Freud e de Lacan para a estética. Lisboa: Faculdade de Belas-Artes da Universidade de Lisboa, 2005. Tese de doutoramento em Belas Artes.

[268] DOWNING, Cristine – Sigmund Freud and the Mythological Tradition. pp. 3-14.

[269] Cf. FREUD, Sigmund – **Essais de psychanalyse**. Paris: Payot, 1979.

GALDSTON, Iago – A Critical Summary and Review. pp. 316-327.

[270] VELLEMAN, J. David – A Rational Superego. pp. 529-558.

JOSEPHNS, Lawrence – The Freudian Superego. pp. 149-151.

beings, undergoing an illusion, the true impulse being forced and constrained by the demands of culture (society)[271]. Even so, psychoanalysis took sublimation to a negative path, in which Freud promised an essay that he never did.

In fact, we cannot answer what man is, but only describe history, anthropology and philosophy for a pragmatic anthropology. In the case of the arts, it involves portraying the human condition, and in Nietzsche and Freud, it was not possible to explain this process of completely disappearing something of appeal, even if latent.

In this way, we can confront the sublimate repression and the shadow repression, and in the first type of repression, the problem lies in the ability to do something bigger and if we are forced to do art and science, or if sublimation responds to something more raised as the question of the "soul" for Plato[272].

So, we can ask a new question: is the sublime real or is it just a mirage? To answer this question, one of the hypotheses would be based on the concept of love, enacted as a cultural illusion and that Freud would have (unreal) animal sexuality. In the Freudian analytical process, the transfer of this process occurs and does not happen at the conscious level, the final result of personal analysis being the "unreal" itself.

On the other hand, from the point of view of finitude, love is something that is most real, being present at the beginning of everything as "God is Love"[273].

---

[271] LIPOVETSKY, Gilles; SERROY, Jean – **A Cultura-Mundo. Resposta a uma sociedade desorientada**. Tradução de Victor Silva. Lisboa: Edições 70, 2010.

[272] HEGEL, G.W.F. – The Philosophy of Plato. pp. 225-268.

[273] A Bíblia Sagrada – I João 4:8 – "Quem não ama não conhece a Deus, porque Deus é amor". Available at http://www.bibliaon.com/versiculo/1_joao_4_8/ [18-05-2015].

About creativity, in historical terms it can be based on concepts related to ingenuity and creation, starting with Plato in his work Ion and only reflected by Nietzsche in his work Human, too human (part 4)[274]. In this way, for Plato, the rhapsody, which would not be art, but poetry, knows how to produce through "mania" (divine), in which poets are possessed by the divine, in a kind of delusion or trance[275].

Even for Kant, on the German concept of Genie, he resorts to the old idea of genius, formed by nature, in which man tends only to the possibility of opening the channel to the fluidity of genius. [276].

The concept of "creating" in Judeo-Christian terms, goes back to the Sumerians and responds to the divine creation of the world, as in Genesis, the original and valuable ideas consist of positive retribution, being all other forms of delusion (private delusion) . On the other hand, it also refers to the ability to innovate, find solutions, know how to solve a problem, discover and create strategies.

If we can consider a history of creativity, it has always been more linked to science and the arts, and more recently, it has branched out into the sphere of public communication and performance.

Creativity can be approached from several perspectives: divine, theological and psychological. Thus, the creative idea has

POLKA, Brayton – 'Freud, Science, and the Psychoanalytical Critique of Religion: The Paradox of Self-Referentiality'. pp. 59-83.

[274] Cf. NIETZSCHE, Friedrich – **Humano, demasiado humano: um livro para espíritos livres**. Lisboa: Relógio D'Água, 1997.

[275] PARTEE, Morriss Henry – Inspiration in the Aesthetics of Plato. pp. 87-95.

HARRIS, John P. – Plato's "Ion" and the End of his "Symposium". pp. 81-100.

[276] WANG, Orrin N.C. – Jant's Strange Light: Romanticism, Preiodicity, and the Catachresis of Genius. pp. 15-37.

its own characteristics, based on innovation and the quality of a given task, becoming relevant. On the other hand, the attitude is based on the desire to do differently, being linked to the personality and dividing into divergent or convergent and open or closed thinking. Finally, this attitude also defends ideals such as non-conformism, attraction to complexity and tolerance to ambiguity.

The creative process must be comprehensive, create stages at the creative and cognitive level, assess its quality, insertion in society, education and accessibility.

In the understanding of creativity in Plato's *Ion*, there would be something of greater interest in finitude and where we find the solutions[277]. However, the work of art is no longer divine and is the result of hard work, in which genius is incessant energy, personal courage, based on education through its own models and methodologies[278]. In this work, Plato understands that the finished work of art has nothing to do with its evolution.

On the other hand, the shadow of creativity is in constant relationship with madness and ethics. In the first, more complex, it is not possible to assess whether madness facilitates the path to creativity, and may even work the other way around, where it only helps delusion (perfection or madness in psychosis). Still on madness, Jung gives the example of James Joyce, where he states that the writer will have stayed on the edges of madness[279].

On the dark side, Francesca Gino gives an example, her creative personality is based on "out of the box" concepts, tending to unethical behavior, cheating and everything that is the

---

[277] *Cf.* PLATÃO – **Íon**. Lisboa: Inquérito, 2000.

[278] Idem, §64.

[279] MCKNIGHT, Jeanne – Unlocking the World-Hoard: Madness, Identity and Creativity in James Joyce. pp. 420-435.

KAPLAN, Robert – Madness and James Joyce. pp. 172-176.

opposite becomes true[280]. Usually this type of behavior is associated with Descartes' "Evil Genius" in relation to Bernard Madoff[281]. Even so, this association between creativity and dishonesty refers to the approach of the dishonest and non-creative.

In human conditioning, there are several factors and ways of overcoming such as the repression of the shadow and the sublime. Socrates, on the other hand, claimed that the new scientists, conscious, remained limited only to what they perceived.

On the other hand, deontology demonstrates the depth of our ignorance, with the example of new technologies, in which the human being has the capacity to receive 11 million bytes per second, processing only 40 bytes of this information[282].

In this way, we can demonstrate that there is more in reality than we know and only with the expansion of our perception and awareness of it, we can in fact increase absorption and increase the conscious capacity for information absorption.

---

[280] GINO, Francesca; PIERCE, Lamar – Lying to Level the Playing Field: Why People May Dishonestly Help or Hurt Others to Create Equity. pp. 89-103.

[281] BOUWSMA, O.K. – Descartes' Evil Genius. pp. 141-151.

KENNINGTON, Richard – The Finitude of Descartes' Evil Genius. pp. 441-446.

GINO, Francesca; WILTERMUTH, Scott S. – **Evil Genius? How Dishonesty Can Lead to Greater Creativity**. Available at http://www.pscience.com/wp-content/uploads/2014/02/EvilGenius.pdf [17-05-2015].

[282] THOMPSON, Herb – Cybersystemic Learning. Radical Pedagogy (2001). Available at http://www.radicalpedagogy.org/radicalpedagogy/Cybersystemic_Learning.html [17-05-2015].

In *Hípias Maior's* work, Plato does not seek to know more, but tries to know what we know in fact[283]. This author also considered the human condition as vertical ignorance, in which we limit ourselves to judge in insufficiency, as a man who has so many certainties and is aware of everything, it is just an illusion and unconscious that Freud and Lacan deepened in their studies[284].

The transversal ignorance, explored by Freud, is based on the early point of the unconscious, being characterized by being a lapse when we talk about sex, death or even identity. In the analytical process, we try to do everything and transfer love to the psychoanalyst, bypassing the blind spot and, thus, not touching the unconscious truth[285].

The psychological approach has several schools, thus demonstrating that there is no consensus on what the psyche is. Human development is not concerned with stories, but with human potential - how far can we go.

Once again, Plato, on the transitive human condition between Ignorance and Wisdom, addresses in his work Banquet, the levels of the Beautiful and criticizes Socrates for not being prepared for the major initiations of this path to Wisdom[286].

On the other hand, through the "allegory of the cave", Plato demonstrates how this path is made up of stages of

---

[283] *Cf.* PLATÃO, op. cit., 1985.

[284] *Cf.* LACAN, Jacques – **O seminário**. Rio de Janeiro: Jorge Zahar Editor, 1995.

FREUD, op. cit., 1979.

[285] PARTNER, Nancy F. – No Sex, No Gender. pp. 419-443.

[286] *Cf.* PLATÃO – **O Banquete**. Lisboa: Edições 70, 1991.

NICHOLS, Mary P. – Philosophy and Empire: On Socrates and Alcibiades in Plato's "Symposium". pp. 502-521.

NICHOLS, Mary P. – Socrates' Contest with the Poets in Plato's Symposium. pp. 184-206.

knowledge with factors that we completely ignore and, in this case, Wisdom and Good would be outside the cave. Self-realization - cave access - is powerful or illusory, with the figure of Socrates being a self-realized figure[287].

In fact, life does not favor stagnation, but rather human discovery, and just like the truth, there is an elimination of the repression of the sublime, and we do not repress the incognito, but the best we have. On the other hand, Jung proposes archetypal repression.

In this way, it will then be necessary to take care not only of the basement, but also of the subkey and also of what is most elevated (psychology of the elevated). Thus, the link between psychoanalysis and psychology goes through Piaget's cognitive development[288], Freud[289] and morale of Culbert.

Finally, the artist's archetype is characterized in the first instance by its dilettante, pedantic, psychotic aspect; in the second instance, as a "transmutator" of the self and the world; in the third instance, as a contemplator; in the fourth instance, as a sage, he becomes a mirror of the archetypal real; finally, curator of the human community.

In conclusion, what escapes us from consciousness is enormous, challenging life about creativity and expressing "lack of definition" and taking us to new parameters in art and science. In this way, it was possible to distinguish creativity as divine inspiration for Plato and genius for Kant.

---

[287] MENN, Stephen – Aristotle and Plato on God as Nous and as the Good. pp. 543-573.

[288] Cf. WADSWAORTH, Barry J. – **Piaget's theory of cognitive and affective development**. 4ª Edição. New York: Longman, 1989.

SCHLEIFER, Michael – Moral Education and Indoctrination. pp. 154-163.

SAXE, Geoffrey B. – Piaget and Anthropology. pp. 136-143.

[289] SIMPSON, Miles – The Sociology of Cognitive Development. pp. 287-313.

On the other hand, the 'transfiguration of the new' for Adorno, is characterized by the work of art and the obligation to introduce something new and intangible[290]. In this way, we can give the example of "abstract novelty", a concept introduced by Fernando Pessoa, leading to what is elevated and sublime[291].

Finally, the connection between the human condition and artistic production must contribute to the search as a process of personal and collective human discovery from the general point of view.

---

[290] GUERLAC, Suzanne – Bataille in Theory: Afterimages (Lascaux). pp. 6-17.

SEEL, Martin – Art as Appearance: Two Comments on Arthur C. Danto's after the End of Art. pp. 102-114.

[291] THOMPSON, Timothy A. – Pórtico partido para o Impossível: Fernando Pessoa and the Portuguese Sublime. pp. 151-168.

Raul Lino

Raúl Lino (1879-1974) presents himself as an innovative architect, with works such as the Tivoli Theater, where the maximum representations of his lines are presented[292].

This author produces for the campaign generated by the Estado Novo, with enormous ideological strand and this author also fights modernism, although he was later considered a modern architect for his time[293].

Raul Lino was born in the context of the Portuguese Monarchy, lives and produces in the Republic, as well as the Estado Novo and still attends the Democratic Regime, starting in 1899 until the 70s of the 20th century.

On the other hand, this architect was part of the group of the General Direction of Building and National Monuments (DGEMN), and the studies of Maria João Neto are essential to understand his involvement with this restoration campaign of the 20th century[294]. This restoration "chain" aimed to remove all the additions made to the monuments after its execution, returning to the "original design" of the same, privileging Gothic and Manueline.

Taking as an example the removal of tile panels from their location as an objective, of a given architectural space,

[292] Cf. GODINHO, Aulo-Gélio Severino – **Raul Lino: o artista e a obra**. Porto: Associação Portuense de Ex-Libris, 1972.

[293] ALMEIDA, Pedro Vieira de – Raul Lino, Arquitecto Moderno. pp. 115-188.

[294] Cf. NETO, Maria João – **James Murphy e o restauro do Mosteiro de Santa Maria da Vitória no Século XIX**. Lisboa: Editorial Estampa, 1996.

NETO, Maria João – Memória, Propaganda e Poder – O Restauro dos Monumentos Nacionais (1929-1960). pp. 253-269.

consequently losing its value when transposed to a museum. On the other hand, the same thing happens in gilded wood, giving the example of the Church of Jesus of Setúbal[295].

In fact, this author is an exceptional case, since he presents a huge bag of History of Art like none of his colleagues of his time, not even the historians of that time[296]. On the other hand, Lino has the conception of architecture in which the territory is fundamental, fitting in with its historical and heritage nature.

There are 677 projects with Raul Lino's descriptive memory at the Gulbenkian Library[297]. This architect not only designed housing buildings, but also a museum and pavilions, as is the case with the Paris Colonial Exhibition, 1931 and also, the Brazilian Pavilion in the Portuguese World. In the case of museums, this architect designed the remodeling of the Museum of Contemporary Art, better known as Museu do Chiado, in Lisbon and the Igreja do Corpo Santo in Setúbal.

On the other hand, this author has recommendations for restoration on the Overseas Historical Archive, Sala Pompeiana and the Hotel de Seteais, in which he seeks to preserve the experiences of these places.

The examples presented in this session were constituted as forms of redefinition and "reframing" of Casa dos Patudos (1904), Santa Maria in Cascais (1902-1918), Cypress trees in Sintra (1912-1914) and Casa da Praia (1920).

---

[295] *Cf.* LINO, Raul, *Projeto de reconstrução dos Paços do Concelho, Setúbal, 1928*, 19 desenhos de arquitetura, 1 desenho técnico de engenharia e memórias descritivas, Arquivo da Fundação da Biblioteca Calouste Gulbenkian.

[296] *Cf.* AA. VV. – **Colóquio Nacional Raul Lino em Sintra, Casa dos Penedos**. Actas do II Ciclo de Conferências, coord. Rodrigo Sobral Cunha, 25 e 26 de Junho de 2004. Sintra: Castelo do Amor, 2014.

[297] Available at http://www.biblartepac.gulbenkian.pt/ [18-05-2015].

In fact, Lino had in-depth knowledge about the most diverse artistic technologies and his basic training was in Decorative Arts. In this way, he will carry out architecture and restoration, in which the latter was only possible with that same knowledge of technologies in the 1940s, that no one else in his time had them - knowing where these traditional technologies are (connection with vernacular architecture).

Raul Lino's problem is based on the question: "What is the museological thinking behind Lino?" And also, "How are projects and rehabilitation carried out according to heritage?".

It is worth noting that Lino was an extraordinary writer, even having a column in the Diário de Notícias, already gathered in a book[298]. On the other hand, his descriptive memories represent the best in Lino, even if some projects do not have a descriptive memory and vice versa. Finally, in the restoration area, it is possible to observe his enormous knowledge of technologies, deepening his relationship with heritage.

This question of a global approach to heritage is derived from Rosalind Krauss' concept of "expanded field"[299], proposing a new postmodern reality applicable to Heritage Studies, where museology, history, science and conservation and restoration work as a whole[300].

Despite his basic training being in Decorative Arts, Lino was a decorative arts technician until he was recognized by the Estado Novo in the 1920s as an architect. On the other hand, it is not possible to explain Lino's work without considering his

---

[298] Cf. CUNHA, Rodrigo Sobral – **Sintra, Raul Lino**. Lisboa: Colares Editora, 2014.

[299] KRAUSS, Rosalind E. – The Originality of the Avant-Garde and other modernist myths. pp. 276-290.

[300] PEREIRA, Fernando António Baptista; DIAS, Fernando Rosa – Ciências da Arte e a Criação Artística: solidariedades para uma investigação em arte. pp. 214-228.

knowledge of history and his training in England and Germany (and not Paris as it was recurring at the time)[301].

In 1902, he made a trip to Morocco, where he immersed himself in the Middle Ages, absorbing its architecture and culture, influencing his work as will be discussed later[302].

On the other hand, Lino had the notion of "Estilo Chão" even before George Kubler coined this concept 60 years later[303]. In a way, Lino transports the history itself and not historicism into the gaze, going to the field to know history and not only through the manuals that are copied from the schools of Fine Arts.

What distinguishes Lino from the 19th century is the realm of "pastiche" (to do it in the manner of ...), appropriate or quoted, as is the example of the Rossio Station, imitated by the Gothic and other styles such as the Neo-Gothic and Neo-Manueline. In the case of Lino, he appropriates his national roots, creating a symbiosis between classical art and vernacular art, although such a mixture at that time was unthinkable.

Even so, he aimed to renovate the houses, with modernization as a fundamental key, constantly citing the Portuguese heritage, leaving aside the Anglo-Saxon influences he drank in his formation.

In his written work Our house of 1918, it is inspired by English architecture, due to Anglo-Saxon influence, translating

[301] *Cf.* LINO, Raul – **Casas Portuguesas: alguns apontamentos sobre o arquitectar das casas simples**. Lisboa: Cotovia, 1992.

[302] *Cf.* RIBEIRO, Irene – **Raul Lino: Pensador Nacionalista da arquitectura**. Lisboa: Faculdade de Arquitectura da Universidade do Porto publicações, 1994.

[303] *Cf.* KUBLER, George – **A arquitectura portuguesa chã: entre as especiarias e os diamantes, 1521-1706**. Lisboa: Vega, 1988.

into Portuguese style[304]. His written work A casa Portuguesa, from 1929, started with the Estado Novo and states Augusto-França that Lino belongs to the 90's generation, linking him to Saudosismo, for being linked to this philosophy. Finally, his written work A nossa casa, from 1918, mentions the importance of knowing geography, geology, history, etc., in order to find the best solution for each case (individualization of cases).

D. José Pessanha, a ceramics scholar, praises Lino's methodology, affirming him as a man ahead of his time, a visionary with a vision requirement for the need to modernize homes without forgetting national roots.

On the other hand, Teixeira de Carvalho, represents his portrait through a modern reflection of all countries based on history. Finally, Ramalho de Ortigão also defended these issues, not only for classical art, but also for vernacular (popular) art[305].

In fact, Lino does not seek to explore the art of the past, but appropriates the past to create the modern, with the example of the "Beethoven" room, where he receives the answer from António Arroio as little Portuguese, Lino himself replying as anonymous that it has nothing to do with German art, looking for Portuguese roots through "self-cooling" - indirectly describing the Chão style.

Summing up Lino's thought to the appropriation of erudite and vernacular history to function fully in Portuguese architecture.

The first example, the Casa dos Patudos, has vernacular elements on the balconies - "ranchas" - and on top of neorromantic columns, making it an apparently revivalist logic on top of a popular balcony.

---

[304] *Cf.* LINO, Raul – **A nossa casa: apontamentos sobre o bom gosto na construção das casas**. Lisboa: Ottosgrafica, 1923.

[305] *Cf.* ORTIGÃO, Ramalho – **O culto da arte em Portugal**. Lisboa: A.M. Pereira, 1896.

On the other hand, the combination of materials such as stone and brick would never be made, for example, by Ventura Terra or José Luís Monteiro. The appropriation of tiles from the 18th century from other places to be placed in the baseboard also demonstrates how Lino knows and understands how to place them. However, Lino will place new tile elements, explicitly designed for that house - heraldic - alluding to the function of the house or the owners.

In this house, he designs a Sala dos Primitiva (1904), where this concept of "primitives" was still new, and also the Sala Renascença, as the first major museology project, where Lino places a skylight in order to allow entry enough light to enjoy works of art. Also regarding these spaces and, in particular, the Gallery, the type of architectural design indicates that Lino would know the Wallace Collection for its similarity.

The second example is the Casa de Santa Maria, in Cascais, from 1902, by order of Mr. Jorge O'Neill. In 1915, it will have a great expansion, after the death of O'Neill and acquisition by José Lino, brother of Raul Lino[306].

The transplanted ceiling for the dining room comes from a church and adapts tiles to spaces identical to those that would have originally been placed, being possible to date them from the 18th century. Nowadays, this ceiling has no religious reading because it covered all religious symbols.

Finally, it is worth noting that Lino's knowledge of technologies allowed for the best choice and solution for building an architecture as he designed it, allowing him to choose the best materials for his own solutions and the best executors for that.

---

[306] *Cf.* AA. VV. – **Casa de Santa Maria em Cascais: Raul Lino**. Cascais: Câmara Municipal, 2005.

Another example is the Casa dos Ciprestes in Sintra, it is a work made for Raul Lino himself, with a more intimate character. In this case, the elements referring to the heritage are tiles and possibly come from the Palácio da Vila.

Intentions of Interior Design, with influences of Jurgen Style, committed to the usual design, appropriates these models. In this house, the entrance is made through a patio and contains an oval room, which grants as neoclassical, as Joanine architecture, Neoclassical Dining Room, this whole structure is based on a quarry with an abrupt slope of the land.

From this place it is possible to see the Pena Palace, the Sintra Village and the Castelo dos Mouros through a single room, which transforms into the center of the identity and magical places of this village.

On the other hand, it also grants a loggia (veranda) in the Renaissance way as a space for reflection and freedom. Still on the oval dining room, it is worth noting that this one, as it is built, contains a perfect sound dimension, with "trompe l'oeil" decorations, and this architectural structure is richly inspired by Franz Adolph Haus.

Casa da Praia, is a work of maximum rusticity, without electricity or running water and in a privileged location, where the Atlantic Ocean enters the entire house, in its natural and scenic dimension. That is, this house is located on a cliff, 60 meters high, with architectural lines expressly vernacular.

In the 1919 museum restoration projects, we have the Beja Convent that was demolished, with works of pastiche and gothic windows in a Manueline building. In this way, Lino eliminates all false elements, demolishing the altar wall of the nuns' separation, creating a larger space, recovering the church's carving (cleaning and re-fixing) and covering Hispano-Arab tiles.

In fact, Lino's attitude is the attitude still practiced today by conservators of built monuments.

On the other hand, we have the project to expand the Museum of Contemporary Art - Museu do Chiado, which has never been completed[307]. Lino designs a modern architecture, with a sober style and without any appropriation, only in the entrances it resorts to the floor style.

On the plan, it is possible to see the indication of the workshops by José Veloso Salgado and Columbano Bordalo Pinheiro, who would be on the lower floor of the Museum, with vertical windows, being Columbano himself director until 1929, succeeding Veloso Salgado in the chair and Sousa Lopes at the museum.

The Colonial Pavilion of Paris, in 1941, has three versions of the same project, in which Lino chooses to build three pavilions linked together, with a tower with the cross of Christ, in order to allow greater visibility of the Pavilion, considering the thick afforestation around it[308].

Lino believed that exterior architecture was essential and showed what was going to happen inside it. In this way, it will bring together 15th century architecture, discoveries, mudéjar, final Gothic and a Manueline portal entirely designed by the same. On the other hand, one of the pavilions was based on tea architecture, citing classicism in this second pavilion. The third and last pavilion is characterized by modern architecture, presenting the products of the Portuguese colonies, similar to the facade of the current Museum of Popular Art.

[307] LINO, Raul – **Projecto de ampliação do Museu de Arte Contemporânea, Rua Serpa Pinto, Lisboa, 1930**. Series of 7 architectural drawings, Archive of the Calouste Gulbenkian Foundation Library. [11-05-2015].

[308] LINO, Raul – **Exposição Colonial Internacional de Paris**. Series of 15 architectural drawings, 4 photographs, program, descriptive memories, specifications, interior decoration of the pavilions and press articles, Archives of the Fundação Calouste Gulbenkian Library. [11-05-2015].

The Brazil Pavilion at Expo do Mundo, in 1939, aims to not relate Portuguese architecture in Brazil, but to meet the essence of that same country. In this way, Lino makes use of nature, translating into the balance of Greek architecture, essentialism and detachment characteristic of this art. Thus, we can observe columns alluding to palm trees, ending in a roof that also alludes to the thick forest, characteristic of the Amazon. In the center of this entrance, we can see a figure that emerges from the earth, gesturing the essence of the whole work, with relation between man-architecture-nature.

Still on matters of restoration, it is worth noting the Casa do Corpo Santo, from 1945, with walls, floors and eaves designed according to the history and geography of that same space.

The 1946 Viana do Castelo Wall, on the other hand, alludes to a retrogression by Lino when he struggled against pastiche and, in a way, ends up concretizing it in this work, with a proposal for four new rooms, with a huge skylight in the center and circulation areas for exhibition.

The Sala Pompeiana, from 1934, in this work Lino uses minimal intervention and respect for traditional materials. Although the Seteais Palace is not a museum - it is a hotel - it follows the principles of the Pompeian Room, but does not advocate the use of old-fashioned furniture, stating that in certain rooms, this furniture must be genuine and in the guest rooms and others, it must be new for the purpose.

In short, Raul Lino had an innovative and updated thought until the mid-twentieth century, with first-rate information at an international level, making individual responses for each case.

Physics research in art

This presentation was divided into 6 fundamental points:

1. Examination and Analysis Methods

1.1. Electromagnetic Spectrum

1.2. Interaction of electromagnetic radiation with matter

2. Ultraviolet fluorescence

3. Infrared reflectography

4. Radiography

5. X-ray fluorescence

6. Conclusion

1. Analytical methods

They represent tools that use different radiations, and through the interaction that these radiations have with the materials, they allow to draw conclusions about these. It is necessary to know about these radiations and what results have been obtained[309].

The methods are divided into examination methods, where the results are obtained through an image and analysis methods, which allow to analyze the chemical composition of our object under study [310].

---

[309] ORTI, Maria Angustias – Los métodos de análisis físico-químicos y la historia del arte. p. 23.

[310] GÓMEZ, Maria Luisa – La restauración: Examen científico aplicado a la conservación de obras de arte. pp. 147-156.

1.1. Electromagnetic spectrum

The radiation of whatever type has a frequency and wavelength (λ) and are related in an inverse way. As the frequency increases, so does your energy.

The information resulting from the application of examination and analysis methods to the object of study, comes from the differentiated interaction of electromagnetic radiation with its matter. The use of electromagnetic radiation of different wavelengths allows us to obtain information about the various stratigraphic levels of the object.

1.1. Interaction of electromagnetic radiation with matter

The dispersion of light is characterized by the way it interacts with the materials of the work. The scattering of light is carried out at various wavelengths. The most dispersed radiation is ultraviolet, and those below this radiation will have less dispersion and other ones will have greater dispersion(x).

If we want to know information about the underlying design, we cannot use ultraviolet radiation because it is scattered over the entire surface of the work, and all the information given to us is at the superficial level.

If we want more in-depth information, infrared radiation - suffers less dispersion - allows information to be obtained at the level of the preparation layers (paint).

2. Ultraviolet fluorescence

The use of UV radiation in the examination of artistic objects dates back to 1925 with the beginning of the Wood lamp[311].

---

[311] *Cf.* RÉNE DE LA RIE, Etienne – Fluorescence of paint and varnish layers (Part I). pp. 1-7.

The UV radiation used in this examination method is between 360 and 400 nm, having photons with sufficient energy to promote electronic excitation processes in the molecules, in which they absorb the radiation and pass to the excited state. When they return to the ground state, radiation characteristic of the compounds present in the sample is emitted[312]. This radiation is emitted in the visible range of the electromagnetic spectrum, being possible to register it with conventional photographic equipment. Fluorescence ceases immediately after removal of the UV light source.

As can be seen in the example below in the work Adoration of the Magi (Trevi, Italy, 1522), ultraviolet radiation can be used to discover that kings, in their robes, presented adornments suited to royal robes, not visible in visible light. .

Ultraviolet radiation is the most important light of the sun, only discovered in 1913 and, commonly, known as black light.

Ultraviolet radiation has enough energy to ionize some molecules, making them go into an excited state and when they return to their fundamental state, they release energy at the level of visible radiation and obtain some information. In examination methods it is known as fluorescence photography induced by ultraviolet radiation.

It is worth noting that to obtain exams with this radiation, it is necessary to use goggles in order to avoid health problems at eye level in the medium and long term.

This radiation makes it possible to detect interventions, and over time, the varnishes fluoresce in a bluish tone, in which all the black areas are the result of a new varnish.

---

[312] SOUSA, Pedro Manuel – Os exames de área na pintura de cavalete e o ensino experimental da Física. p. 11.

This technique can be used in the most varied areas, giving an example in sculpture, in which an excerpt from the hand of Venus Genetrix do Louvre suffered.

In this way, it is possible to conclude that different fluorescence corresponds to different materials. On the other hand, in Picasso's work, infrared reflectography, allowed to discover a work that was looking for The Old Guitarist and also allowed to identify that he used charcoal drawings and the guitar strings. Even so, these conclusions were only possible from documentation, namely letters between Picasso and Jacó[313].

3. Infrared reflectography

Infrared radiation is obtained with just one lamp, having been discovered in the 1800s, but only in the 1930s was it applied in art[314]. What distinguishes it from the photograph is the spectral range 900 nm - 2000 nm, they can penetrate even more in the work, and the detection is possible through a specific system that blocks visible light and only allows the recording of infrared radiation[315].

In the IR reflectography technique, the radiation is recorded using specific sensors, blocking the entry of visible radiation through the application of filters specifically designed

---

[313] See more at http://vangoghletters.org/vg/letters/let688/letter.html [21-04-2015].

[314] *Cf.* DORRELL, Peter – **Photography in archaeology and Conservation**. Cambridge: Cambridge University Press, 1989.

MATTEINI, Mauro; MOLES, Arcangelo – **Scienza e restauro**. Firenze: Nardini Editore, 1984.

MAIRINGER, Franz – The ultraviolet and fluorescence study of paintings and manuscripts. pp. 40-55.

Idem – UV-, IR- and X-ray imaging. pp. 15-71.

[315] *Cf.* FARIES, Molly – Analytical capabilities of infrared reflectography: an art historian's perspective. pp. 87–104.

HAIN, Miraslov et al. – Multispectral analysis of cultural heritage artefacts. Measurement Science Review. Vol. 3, n° 1 (2003), pp. 9–12.

for this purpose. The resulting image - reflectogram - is presented in white and black, translating the contrast between the diffused radiation (white) and the absorbed radiation (black) by the materials used in the execution of the work[316].

This technique has the added value of being noninvasive, non-destructive and due to the portability of the equipment, it can be used in situ, without the need to move the works[317].

Since the Middle Ages, artists have carried out a preparatory drawing with a brush, charcoal, graphite or pencil to define the forms and compositions of the paintings. The observation of this underlying drawing, characteristic of a certain painter, can allow to standardize and in this way to specifically characterize his technique. These drawings can be essential for art historians due to the important information for identifying painters and production workshops[318].

4. Radiography

In the case of radiography, at the Kröller-Müller Museum, about a painting by Van Gogh, there was documentation that both proved that this work was of the painter as it was not, so

---

[316] STUART, Barbara – Analytical Techniques in Materials Conservation. p. 73.

[317] Cf. FARIES, Molly – Analytical capabilities of infrared reflectography: an art historian's perspective. pp. 87–104.

HAIN et al, op. cit., pp. 9–12.

ASPEREN DE BOER, J.R.J. – Infrared reflectography: A method for the examination of paintings. pp. 1711–1714.

[318] Cf. STUART, op. cit., p. 73.

LORENA, Mercês et al. – O desenho dentro da pintura do tríptico de Coimbra. p. 68.

RODRIGUES, Maria Dalila Aguiar – Modos de expressão na pintura portuguesa: O processo criativo de Vasco Fernandes (1500-1542). Coimbra: Faculdade de Letras da Universidade de Coimbra, 2000. Dissertação de Doutoramento.

ORTI, op. cit., p. 41.

this technique was used, which also came to reveal another little work " van Gogh's typical style. However, through a letter in particular between Van Gogh and his brother, the latter asked for the work in exchange for money, in which Van Gogh sends the work underneath as proof that he was producing.

The discoverer of X radiation was Wilhelm Röentgen (1845-1923), discharging energy into an ampoule, but as it was not possible to observe anything with the naked eye, he placed an aluminum foil and a barium salt card at the end of the ampoule, making it possible observe fluorescence with this radiation[319].

On the other hand, he also realized that this radiation penetrated different materials. Then, with his wife's hand, he took the first X-ray.

In the case of radiography, we put a film behind the work, when it transmits in the area of the work where it absorbs, it becomes whiter, where it passes, it gets dark, allowing to obtain interesting results[320].

A recent case of this application is the work *O Eremita* by António DaCosta, from 1925, where the radiography allowed to observe the presence of a work that was looking for its whereabouts[321].

5. X-ray fluorescence

The principle of the X-ray fluorescence technique is to use an X radiation source to ionize the innermost layers of atoms.

[319] TOLEDO-PEREYRA, Luis H. – X-Ray Surgical Revolution. pp. 327-332.

[320] PEASE, Murray – A Note on the Radiography of Paintings. pp. 136-139.
CASALI, Franco – X-Ray Digital Radiography and Computed Tomography for Cultural Heritage. pp. 24-28.

[321] FRAGOSO, Diana et al.– *Through The Hermit - Rediscovering António Dacosta's lost painting*, Comunicação Oral Technart 2015, 27-30 de abril, Catânica, Itália.

When an X-ray photon is placed on a sample, it will pull an atom from the innermost layer, creating a gap. As all matter naturally seeks to return to its fundamental state, an atom from an outermost layer will transition to that layer, emitting a photon corresponding to the difference in energies of these two layers. This resulting photon is detected and processed in the form of a spectrum[322].

This radiation allows to know crystalline structures, mammograms, radiographs, used in metal detectors in airports and in the cultural heritage. On the other hand, there are several ranges of this radiation, if we want information on denser materials, higher radiation ranges are used.

When these photons interact with the innermost layers of the atom, it forms a gap that is covered by an atom of an outermost layer, forming a transition between atomic levels and, consequently, the difference in energies gives rise to a photon with energy characteristic of that transition [323]. Thus, by obtaining this characteristic energy, we can know which elements of the periodic table are present in this material - chemical composition of the materials.

In this spectrum, the position of the peaks, read on the abscissa, allows the identification of the elements (from the periodic table) present in the sample. The number of counts for each peak, read in the ordinate, allows determining the quantity of each element present in a sample / object.

[322] MARKOWICZ, Andrzej – Interaction of photons with matter. pp. 17-21.

[323] MATTEINI, Mauro; MOLES, Arcangelo – **La química en la restauración – Los Materiales del arte Pictórico**. San Sebastián: Editorial Nerea, 2001.

CRUZ, António João – A matéria de que é feita a cor. Os pigmentos utilizados em pintura e a sua identificação e caracterização. pp. 1-25.

AA. VV. – **La pintura al temple, Introducción general al arte**. Madrid: Ed. Istmo, 1980, pp. 252-257.

This objective peak / element reading is universally consultable in databases with a numbering system (nomenclature) such as Siegbahn and IUPAC[324].

To exemplify what was being given, the example of the famous Vermeer forger - Han van Meegeren - was given, whose expert process was based on the identification of the element cobalt (Co) in blue (cobalt blue), which appeared only in the 19th century[325]. Bearing in mind that Johannes Vermeer is a 17th century Flemish painter, this pigment did not yet exist, but the ultramarine blue, which was the painter's favorite blue pigment[326].

With this example it was possible to perceive the applicability of the X-ray fluorescence technique, also being given as an example, still on the production of this counterfeiter, the absence of silver (Ag) and antimony (Sb), impurities present in lead white, given the manual production of this pigment[327].

The X-ray fluorescence allows to identify the chemical composition of a sample, all elements of the periodic table above $Z > 12$ (Mg).

Simultaneous analysis of the elements in the sample, non-destructive, portable, in situ, fast and inexpensive.

From the identification of photons, characteristic of the elements of the periodic table, we can determine their presence. On the other hand, the peak area allows to identify the quantity

---

[324] Fonte: http://old.iupac.org/reports/V/spectro/partVIII.pdf [13-12-2014].

[325] COVEY, Preston K. – Art or Forgery? The Strange Case of Han Van Meegeren. p. 2-31.

[326] See more at http://www.nationalgallery.org.uk/paintings/research/meaning-of-making/vermeer-and-technique/vermeers-palette [20-01-2015].

[327] Forgery. Dutchman who painted Vermeers. Available at http://webartacademy.com/forgery-dutchman-who-painted-vermeers [15-12-2014].

of this material. Considering the elements there, we can get an idea of the pigments that are there. The temporal location will depend on its existence or not.

As a disadvantage, the fact that it is elementary, such as malachite green and verdigris, are both compounds of Cu, with this technique it is not possible to know which of the greens, so we have to resort to molecular analysis.

The equipment is portable or bench-top, being the example of the mapping of an Indian miniature studied by the author (despite not being aware of the application of this exam in it), that the white zone is made with barium and the chrome yellow with Pb[328].

An example was also given of a polychrome sculpture in papier-mache, upholstered, with Ca primer, red Fe bole, sheet from another bole and, finally, burnished, applying paint and scraping to get the effect. Through the mapping all layers were confirmed and it was also verified that the upholstery technique had been used.

On the other hand, there are also portable equipment from Bruker, given the example of bronze statuettes, which allowed to know the provenance and age by comparison with other data acquired from similar pieces, being from Alcácer do Sal and Évora, a group of ex -votes, from the Iron Age, analyzing and quantifying their alloy, confirming their similarity, are from a time and source.

Another example was the Manueline charms, illuminated in gold and silver, using the XRF technique, it was possible to confirm the silver and the bronze that is not part of the silver, but the decomposition of this material to the exposure of light. Methyl bromide was used as a fungicide to prevent pests, this

---

[328] CARDEIRA, Ana Mafalda et al. – Spectroscopic characterizatio of a contemporary Indian miniature painting. pp. 1376-1381.

degradation has to do with the chlorine of the parchment production, sodium chloride, together with silver, is extremely photosensitive[329].

The last example of this technique was Archimedes' Polimpsest writings, in which his work was scraped and reused, constituting the only copies of his work. Using the ultraviolet radiation, the fluorescence of the materials is different, so that the contrast between the ink and the parchment is possible, it was possible to see the text written below. These prayer books were illuminated, with gold leaf, using X-ray fluorescence it was possible to map, so Fe was sought, because of the paints, and Archimedes' writings were also found underneath. For better understanding, William Noel's video: Revealing Archimedes' Lost Codex was viewed, within the scope of TEDxSummit 2012[330].

6. Conclusions

In conclusion, the methods of examination and analysis give historians information about the methodology, material composition and lost works, answering material and technical questions, valuing the investigation and allowing identification of false ones.

This session also had a practical component, using the ®Dino-Lite equipment to visualize the materials (crayons, blue pen and charcoal) and their interaction with ultraviolet and infrared radiation.

---

[329] MANSO, Marta et al. – The mysterious halos in iron gall ink manuscripts: an analytical explanation. DOI: 10.1007/s00339-014-8924-z

[330] See more at https://www.ted.com/talks/william_noel_revealing_the_lost_codex_of_archimedes?language=pt [21-04-2015].

As they have not been registered, examples of their application can be consulted in the author's master's dissertation[331].

[331] CARDEIRA, Ana Mafalda – Caracterização material e técnica das 'Académias de nu' de José Veloso Salgado, pertencentes à colecção da FBAUL. Lisboa: Faculdade de Belas-Artes da Universidade de Lisboa, 2014, pp. 75-82. Dissertação de Mestrado em Ciências da Conservação, Restauro e Produção de Arte Contemporânea

Technology, imagery and cyber art

"Cybernetics" is a word created by Norbert Wiener in 1948, defining it as "the scientific study of control and communication in the animal ant the machine"[332].

The "technological wandering" is characterized by being an underground universe regarding the aspects of using new technologies to build an artistic discourse[333]. That is, it uses computers that define themselves as a "non-person", "non-place" and anonymous to make the artistic work visible[334].

In fact, art is a form of knowledge and is totally linked to research in a random and unverifiable way. In this way, Marc Chagall (1887-1985) serves as an example and the representation of objects hovering in the abstract.

Artistic methodologies are individualized and subject to subjectivity. Thus, the question of "why?" Is difficult to answer, requiring the artist to flank to escape these types of questions.

A strategy with elementary appropriations, such as the use of image, shape and color treatment programs, the appropriation of artistic strategies[335].

---

[332] Cf. WIENER, Norbert – Cybernetics. New York: John Wiley & Sons, Inc., 1948.

Idem – Cybernetics or Control and Communication in the Animal and the Machine. Cambridge: MIT Press, 1961.

[333] APTER, Michael J. – Cybernetics and Art. pp. 257-265.

ASCOTT, Roy – Towards a Field Theory for Post-Modernist Art. pp. 51-52.

[334] FERRÃO, Hugo – Ciberespaço e a arquitectura dos "não lugares" habitados por "homens sem qualidades". pp. 179-190.

[335] HERTZ, Paul – Art, Code, and the Engine of Change. pp. 58-75.

BIRRINGER, Johannes – Performance and Science. pp. 22-35.

"Cadavre exquis" consists of an object of circulation and had to be represented, being passed by others without them having knowledge of what was done previously[336].

New technologies also make it possible to desert these digital matrix strategies and, therefore, it is necessary to recover these matrices to carry out an artistic work.

Yves Klein (1928-1962) uses the trace as a handprint, relating this gesture to the fact that we have a very short period of existence.

Art and Science

In the second half of the twentieth century, there is a great seduction on the part of the artists, in which often due to the absence of a theoretical corpus, looking very much at the production of scientific knowledge[337]. In this way, appropriation of this same aspect makes artists more attentive to scientific knowledge. On the other hand, technical production, thinking, creative processes and the artists' masters work and, in this way, a close connection between the universe of science and art grows[338].

"Alternative Zero", in 1977, proves that Portugal was attentive to modernity. This also means that we have been aware of the contemporary context in Europe and America[339].

---

[336] GROSSMAN, Kathryn M. – Playing Surrealist Games: Parataxis and Creativity. pp. 700-707.

APOSTOLIDÈS, Jean-Marie – Du Surréalism à l'Internationale situationniste: la question de l'image. MLN. pp. 727-749.

[337] FERRÃO, Hugo – Imersão tecnológica e desertificação metafísica, ilhas e arquipélagos românticos. pp. 152-163.

[338] FERRÃO, Hugo – A cibercultura e os desafios das novas aprendizagens. pp. 60-66.

[339] NOGUEIRA, Isabel – Alternativa Zero (1977): o reafirmar da possibilidade da criação. pp. 9-28.

Cyberart, a new "techno" look

Curious field, more and more we are open to reading virtual works, in a generation based on fast reading where quickly scan the documents, mimicking the workings of the machines[340]. In other words, we work through blocks of content and, in a way, we are in the heads of the machines. With this, there will be a new space-time relationship.

In heritage terms, the application of software as virtual reconstruction aids has been carried out, giving as an example the project carried out for the Giza Plateau, in Egypt[341].

The notion of space varies according to categories, such as tradition or modernity. Others, in the past, were more holistic, now in modernity it is more segmented. In other words, construction of the 3rd block - storage of information that we previously had as a civilization to do so and in fact, access to information has never been greater than it is today[342].

In the 1970s, Americans thought about mapping the world and today we have the possibility to reconstruct and propose reconstructions in the most varied areas of knowledge, being given as an example in the context of the nucleus, the 3D reconstruction of a painting.

FILIPE, Patrícia Trindade – Alternatica um: Respostas Polémicas à Alternativa Zero. Lisboa: Faculdade de Belas-Artes da Universidade de Lisboa, 2008. Dissertação de Mestrado em Estudos Curatoriais.

[340] POLLOCK, John L. – What Am I? Virtual Machines and the Mind/Body Problem. pp. 237-309.

FERRÃO, Hugo – Mitologia tecnológica: Cyberart – discurso Cyberpunk. pp. 60-69.

[341] Fonte: http://giza3d.3ds.com/#discover [01-06-2015].

[342] DERUYVER, Debra; EVANS, Jennifer – Digital Junction. pp. 943-980.

MCGANN, Jerome – Culture and Technology: The Way We Live Now, What Is to Be Done?. pp. 71-82.

The territoriality of the impossible represents all this content that has lost its space frontier in the world and tends to be the consciousness of beings inhabiting the planet, with artists having a dilutive role in those same borders.

In fact, an artist who wants to carry out an installation needs to speak to an architect, a sound engineer, etc., with Leonel Moura as an example about the transversality of artist production in the various fields of science and technology, given as an example[343].

In fact, a new phenomenological discussion about the virtual world appears. However, in the first instance, it is necessary to know what is virtual and what is the virtual world. On the other hand, it is a fact that "the virtual" is not sensitive, but despite this, our brain begins to have difficulties in discerning what is real and virtual.

Still on fiction / reality, the Blade Runner film is given as an example, from fiction to reality[344].

Artists who reduce the scheme of privatizing the body in its entirety is a form of expression, taking this type of communication as the ability to inform or misinform certain groups. Even so, nowadays, an artist needs to be linked to an institution in order to have strength and projection of his production.

[343] MEANS, Loren – Autonomous Robots That Paint. pp.. 2-14.

[344] MCNAMARA, Kevin R. – "Blade Runner's" Post-Individual Worldspace. pp. 422-446.

FERRÃO, Hugo – Pintura como hipertexto do visível: instauração do tecno-imaginário do citor. Lisboa: Faculdade de Belas-Artes da Universidade de Lisboa, 2007. Tese de Doutoramento em Belas-Artes, especialidade de Pintura.

KLEIN, Norman M. – Building Blade Runner. pp. 147-152.

YU, Timothy – Oriental Cities, Postmodern Futures: "Naked Lunch, Blade Runner", and "Neuromancer". pp. 45-71.

On the other hand, our world increasingly wants the hypertext format, giving as an example Ted Nelson, in which he defends that in the near future, we will read and write everything in the planned world, focusing our activity on the computer and communication networks[345]. One of the first creators of hypertext prototypes in Portugal was the speaker[346], in which he took the life of Rocha de Sousa and transformed it into hypertext, forming it into layers. In other words, structures in nodes and connections, crossing paths with multimedia[347].

In fact, there is a lot of fiction around man-made machines, starting with William Gibson's fantastic work *Neuromancer*[348]. Another example, the Guggenheim building in Bilbao, is a kind of ship-ship, being looked at as a machine. On the one hand, in an aerial view, its organic aspect can be observed, but underneath, there are projected fairs.

Bioarte, giving itself as an example Stelarc (1946-) - "the body I have can be improved" - presents himself as an artist who

[345] *Cf.* NELSON, Thedor – **Computer Lib / Dream Machines**. New York: Microsoft edition, 1987.

WARDRIP-FRUIN, Noah – Hypermedia, Eternal Life, and the Impermanence Agent. pp. 353-358.

BOLTER, Jay David – The Computer, Hypertext, and Classical Studies. pp. 541-545.

[346] FERRÃO, Hugo – Hipertexto, axis mundi das manifestações tecno-artísticas <u>Arte Teoria</u>. Vol. 1, No. 6 (2005), pp. 31-40.

[347] FERRÃO, Hugo – Invisible network, novas fronteiras artísticas da interação com superfícies e objectos inteligentes. pp. 49-59.

[348] JONES, Gwyneth – Art, Forward Slash, Science. pp. 526-529.

MERRITT, Richard K. – From Memory Arts to the New Code Paradigm: The Artist as Engineer of Virtual Information Space and Virtual Experience. pp. 403-408.

SPONSLER, Claire – Cyberpunk and the Dilemmas of Postmodern Narrative: The Example of William Gibson. pp. 625-644.

seeks ideal canons and makes use of biology to reach them[349]. Another example, the Survival Lab, which consists of a space for groups of artists to use military remains to make shows (1970s) and also, the Robotik Installation, where the greater use of the field of robotics and the modeling of a virtual space is perceived.

Another extremely recognized artist in the field of Bioarte is Eduardo Kac and his production that links living beings and art[350]. On the other hand, one of the Portuguese artists is Pedro Henriques, with the use of technological icons and scattered throughout the faculty.

[349] DIXON, Deborah P. – Creating the Semi-Living: On Politics, Aesthetics and the More-than-Human. pp. 411-425.

[350] ESTÉVEZ, Alberto T. – The Genetic Creation of Bioluminescent Plants for Urban and Domestic Use. pp. 18-19.

YOUNGS, Amy M. – The Fine Art of Creating Life. pp. 377-380.

TOMASULA, Steve – Genetic Art and the Aesthetics of Biology. pp. 137-144.

Digital experience and painting

The crisis and death of painting and crises related to the death of painting[351]. In fact, there is a suffering in the field of pictorial production, looking for an ontological reconfiguration that involves color, shape, etc. and it is based on conceptual issues that were not considered painting before.

In this way, we began to observe an increasingly hybrid configuration, where the internal questioning of painting comes to give a limitation that has emerged over time. If painting is painting, it had a destiny that is not the same as literature or theater and "being and not being" [painting] ceases to be specific and becomes part of what is not specific.

One of the critical moments has been due to its relationship with technologies and sciences, in which this emphasis turns out to be critical in digital image and network communication. In the History of Art, we are aware that the relationship of impressionists with the creation of photography, led them to try to treat what was not photographable, such as color and time. On the other hand, the portability of the creative process emerges through the development of paint tubes, which allowed for greater spontaneity and speed in the process.

Before the discovery of X-rays[352] and the creation of microscopy, leads to the development of futurism. Before cinema, painters are more interested in the moment, making it

---

[351] DANTO, Arthur C. – The End of ARt: A Philosophical Defense. pp. 127-143.

HOWE, Susan – The End of Art. pp. 2-7.

HILMER, Brigitte – Being Hegelian after Danto. pp. 71-86.

[352] Abordada no **subcapítulo 2.1.3**.

expressive in another moment, as well as artificial light[353]. In fact, much of futurism is based on these issues. In this way, through new technologies, non-real images come to be represented and deviate from nature and copy, looking for expressive, impressionistic and abstract potential.

Industrialization and *ready-made[354]*, they unfolded the representation, suggesting a second reality and in this way, made possible the new criticism, such as that of constructivism and the new vanguards. In fact, new thoughts based on the eternal and immutable lead to the appearance of symptoms linked to human organicity, constant metamorphosis and physicality.

In this way we can present three moments: 1st visible, 2nd incomplete experience and 3rd manipulation of the visible.

Some attempts throughout the 20th century, tried through ways of painting that are not based on more traditional forms such as the use of acid or urine, giving as an example the works of Gustav Metzger (1926-) and Andy Warhol (1928-1987). On the other hand, the works of Roxy Paine (1966-), PMU (Painting Machine Unit) from 1999/2000, machines that paint and paint, producing a long history and objects that come close to reality.

Leonel Moura (1948-), Warm paintings, 2001, presents painting robots that work through different configurations based on a digital device, representing the path of ants (random).

---

[353] AIKEN, Edward – The Cinema and Italian Futurist Painting. pp. 353-357.

NORDEN, Martin F. – The Avant-Garde Cinema of the 1920s: Connections to Futurism, Precisionism, and Suprematism. pp. 108-112.

CERONI, Vittori – When Future Met Its Past (The "Futurism" of Filippo T. Marinetti). pp. 665-673.

[354] NESBIT, Molly – Ready-Made Originals: The Duchamp Model. pp. 53-64.

On the other hand, another Portuguese artist, Miguel Palma (1964-), in his work 80.000V for Leonardo Da Vinci, 2007, consisting of an electrical device, with two terminals, that produce electrical discharge and connect two Da Vinci catalogs.

Philip Couton (1961-), The Line of 1978, mirror between art and technology, the painter is a human being, which defines an ontology of painting when the limits are blurred between human and machine.

Finally, Eduardo Kac (1962-) and his various DNA manipulation works, whose relationship is based on the search for a perfect body, in which nothing is what it appears.

Tears in the rain

Studio Azzurro[355], in 2012, he created the work Ombri di passaggio for the São Paulo Biennial. This work consists of an interactive installation, in which the person enters a place where the shadow is not his, but manipulation of a kind of Pinocchio.

On the other hand, Steven Spielberg (1946-), Artificial Intelligence, from 2001, the character David, like the pinocchio (where this story is even used in the argument), he wants to be a real boy and not just an android. And yet, the fact that this is the only witness of the human race.

From Ridley Scott (1937-), the 1986 Blade Runner film, whose completely artificial creatures are so perfect that they have emotions. However, in an act of surprise, of humanity, it is created at the moment the villain dies and with it all the memory that he harvested while he was alive disappears.

At this point, we can raise the question of machine and non-machine, what is post-human and "post-machine life" of integrating into our lives?

---

[355] Available at http://www.studioazzurro.com/ [03-06-2015].

Jean Baudrillard (1929-) addresses questions about seduction and how to undress the ghost of the dream, 1979[356]. In fact, this is a cold seduction, of low intensity, very diluted, where it is necessary to seek high seduction, more sophisticated than philosophical thought.

Jean-François Leyotard (1924-1998), in 1988, publishes a work in which he raises questions such as "if you can land in body?", Stating that nature is interlocutor and that the sun is about to disappear[357].

On the other hand, the human brain does not think of literary, but hypothetical and empirical configurations. Not presenting a code that establishes, in a non negligent way, what is peripheral. It is not focused, but "analogous" to Greek, which means what it looks like, but it is not the same.

Nikoleta Kerinska (1972-), in her work *Art et intelligence artificielle: dans le contexte d'une expérimentation artistique*, addresses questions about the interaction with verbal language and its relationship with artistic image[358].

On the other hand, Slavoj Zizek (1949-), in the work Organs without bodies, questions how the mouse experiences its movement actions, from the application of a brain implant[359].

Finally, Edmund Couchot (1932-) publishes several works where he addresses the issues of image time and machines as a

[356] *Cf.* BAUDRILLARD, Jean – **De la Séduction**. Paris: Galilée, 1979.

[357] *Cf.* LYOTARD, Jean-François – **L'inhumain**. Paris: Galilée, 1988.

[358] KERINSKA, Nikoleta – Art et intelligence artificielle: dans le contexte d'une expérimentations artistique. Paris: Univeristé Sorbonne, Panthéon, 2014. Tese de doutoramento em Ciências da Arte.

[359] ZIZEK, Slavoj – **Organs without bodies**, Available at http://www.lacan.com/zizsalsagon.html [12-06-2015].

means of communicating in art[360]. Although the body is fixed and not human, it is easy to privilege the visual - "sensory" - new technologies are better able to produce the sensory. In this way, we can obtain a new percetual matrix, whose new imagery coincides with the dream.

While it rains or gets sunny

In this last part of the session, it was possible to observe several artistic works based on digital media, starting with David Rokeby (1960-), *San Marco flow* of 2005, where he combines his engineering knowledge with artistic production, representing St. Mark's Square, in Venice.

The work of Jean-Pierre Yvaral, *Mona Lisa synthétisée* of 1982, an image made up of other images. Another example is Scott Draves, *Electric Sheep*, 1999, produces images from the mouse and keyboard[361].

Joseph Nachvatal (1934–2002), exhibition in Paris 2010, despite working on the computer, no time, where the paintings are assisted by computers and result from a computer virus[362]. These works appear as absorbent canvases, transmitting a mysterious side because it seems natural and are extremely appealing to the touch.

Finally, other examples of artists such as Camille Utterback (1970-), Miguel Chevalier (1959-), Peter Greenaway (1965-) and Kutluğ Ataman (1961-) were given.

[360] *Cf.* COUCHOT, Edmond – **Des Images du temps et des machines dans les arts et la communication**. Paris: Éditions Jacquiline Chambon, 2007.

Idem – **L'Art numérique**. Paris: Flammarion, 2003.

Idem – **Tecnologie dans l'art de la photographie a la realité virtuelle**. Paris: Éditions Jacqueline Chambon, 1998.

[361] See more at http://scottdraves.com/sheep.html [12-06-2015].

[362] See more at http://www.eyewithwings.net/nechvatal/ [12-06-2015].

Proportion studies

No hay mejor assunto para los artistas que el cuerpo
humano. Es (...) el elemento de expresión artística más
importante que pueda encontrar-se, y su desnudo, además,
nuestro principal vínculo con las disciplinas clásicas[363].

The study of the nude and the application of anatomy had already been widely addressed, and its application was mutually positive[364]. That is, in an artistic context, the study of anatomy is essential to the representation of the human (or animal) body and, reversing the process, scientific illustration is essential to the study of anatomy by scientists and other scholars in need of such science.

---

[363] CLIMENT, Carlos Plasencia; LANCE, Manuel Martínez – Las proporciones humanas y los cánones artísticos. p. 7.

[364] *Cf.* Idem, 2007.

AA.VV. – **Figures du corps : Une leçon d´anatomie à l´école des Beaux-Arts**. Paris: ENSBA – École des Beaux Arts de Paris, 2008.

AA.VV. – **A permanência do corpo: academias da escola de Lisboa**. Lisboa: Reitoria da Universidade de Lisboa, 1999.

BARCSAY, Jenö – **Anatomía artística del cuerpo humano**. Barcelona: Idea Books, D. L., 1996.

MOREAUX, Arnould – **Anatomia artistica del hombre : compendio de anatomia osea y muscular**. Madrid: Ediciones Norma, 1988.

ANTUNES, João Lobo – **Anatomia: arte e ciência**. Lisboa: fundação Champalimaud, 2013.

MESQUITA, Marilisa – O sorriso humano. Lisboa: Faculdade de Belas-Artes de Lisboa, 2012. Dissertação de Mestrado em Anatomia Artística.

FARIA, Alberto – A Colecção de Desenho Antigo da Faculdade de Belas-Artes de Lisboa (1830-1935): tradição, formação e gosto. Lisboa: Faculdade de Belas-Artes de Lisboa, 2009, 3 vols. Dissertação de Mestrado em Museologia e Museografia.

BERNARDO, José Viriato – A coleção de escultura da Faculdade de Belas Artes: a formação do gosto e o ensino do desenho. Lisboa: Faculdade de Belas-Artes de Lisboa, 2014, 2 vols. Tese de doutoramento em Belas-Artes, especialidade de Desenho.

Still, it is worth noting that the word proportion is the result of the contraction of *"pro"* and *"portion"*, that is, according to a part. In other words, the relationship of a part to the whole, established in a mathematical way and obeying different criteria throughout the history of art[365].

Even before briefly presenting some of the most important canons, the word kanon means "rule" and "precept", being a concrete rule that establishes ideal proportions for the human body with a view to artistic representation[366]. Other definitions can be presented here, but are not justified for the purpose of this report.

The application of anatomy in art comes from an opposite and reciprocal need, integrating itself in illustration in the field of Medicine, forming over time as a reciprocal need for visual representation[367].

> *Póde dizer-se que essa preoccupação vae quasi até á actualidade, e que só recentemente é que as anatomias, especialmente destinadas aos artistas, não se occupam fortuitamente de secções cirurgicas ou medicas. É no seculo XVIII que começam os tratados essencialmente artisticos, mas todos prejudicados por incorrecções, quer de texto, quer de desenho. No seculo XIX, as Anatomias plasticas começam a occupar-se, de fórma mais scientifica e mais preoccupadamente esthetica, das proporções do côrpo humano, da marcha, das attitudes e da exteriorisação das modificações mimicas[368].*

---

[365] CLIMENT, op. cit., p. 17.

[366] Idem, p. 18.

[367] HARCOURT, Glenn – Andreas Vesalius and the Anatomy of Antique Sculpture. pp. 28-61.

SHAW, Joyce Sutler – "The Anatomy Lesson": The Body, Technology and Empathy. pp. 29-38.

[368] LOMBARDINI, A. – Manual de Anatomia Plastica. p. XIX.

The title of this chapter is based on the inversion of the process already presented in the form of an article, where the "beyond the visible" represented the analytical study of material and technical characterization of paintings.

In other words, what is intended, which is largely overlooked by scholars in analytical scientific analysis, is to resume looking at the very surface of painting and representation that is incorporated into it. Moreover, resort to the virtual domain of painting to assist us in the analysis of the work.

The aid of multimedia tools is essential in the survey of this study. In a first step, the photographic registration is carried out in the reserve, so as not to remove the works from their environment (reserve). To obtain these images, the painting is placed on an easel at 90º with the floor, the camera (®Canon 5D + objective EF 24-105mm f / 4L IS USM) is placed at the average height of the painting and at 90º, a scale of ash at the level of the painting surface and two sources of natural light at 45º with the center of the painting.

In a second step, ®Photoshop CS6 is used to crop the image and treat the color level. On the other hand, this software also proved to be useful for calculating the proportion of the head, that is, the dimension that goes from the apex of the skull to the calcaneus region of the foot (extremity of the lower limb) on the human head and, in this case, of paintings performed at the same time by different authors - representing the same model in different views.

Finally, in order to confirm these dimensions, the ®InDesign CS6 software was used, using a grid of equal measures from the tip of the apex of the skull to the calcaneus of the foot (extremity of the lower limb). This proportion analysis is governed by the methodology used to remove the head module and compare it with the total body size of the model[369].

In this chapter, we will try to demonstrate the argumentative support for supporting a canon theory used in the paintings resulting from a competition for the position of Professor of Painting at the School of Fine Arts in Lisbon, in 1934, where Abel Manta (1888-1982) competed. , Fernando dos Santos (1892-1965), Henrique Franco (1883-1961), João Reis (1899-1982) and Bensaúde (unknown). In this contest Henrique Franco was the winner, having been promoted as early as that year[370].

The analysis of the paintings begins at the compositional level, noting that the paintings were made in the same space and time (contest), representing different views of the same model, all made in oil on canvas, with similar dimensions of 100 x 80 cm (present in Room 3.13 and the painting by Fernando dos Santos is in Room 3.41).

In structural terms, it is possible to observe that all painters resorted to the centralization of the model in the pictorial plane. On the other hand, if we assume that none of the paintings had changed in terms of dimensions, Santos and Franco's paintings are positioned slightly above the horizontal level at the center of the composition.

In terms of pictorial structural construction, it is possible to observe a greater dexterity prior to the fitting of the model in the composition by Reis and Bensáude, and Manta's painting is also well thought out at the pictorial level.

In terms of color and tone, it is possible to divide the paintings by their backgrounds and models, balancing the

---

[369] CLIMENT, op. cit., p. 19.

[370] *Cf.* CÂMARA MUNICIPAL DO FUNCHAL – Museu Henrique e Francisco Franco. p. 6.
FARIA, op. cit., p. 151.

ultimate result through conjugation and reciprocal tonal relationship.

In relation to the models, we can observe a majority of choice for the lighter tones, apart from Reis which presents a more yellowish flesh tone. However, it is worth noting that this yellowish hue may be related to the oxidation of the varnish, resulting in the yellowing and darkening of the painting.

At the fund level, it is possible to distinguish several different shades attributed to the funds executed by the painters. In this way, we have bluish tones by Manta, Franco and Bensaúde and brown tones by Santos and Reis.

In plastic terms, we can carry out an initial analysis and measure at the model level and at the bottom level, these two planes being predominant in the compositions. On the one hand, we have a painting at the level of the faintest brushstroke by Santos and Reis and a painting demarcated by the stain in the paintings by Manta, Franco and Bensaúde. However, in terms of backgrounds, all painters present contrasting backgrounds, in order to highlight the model and are all made based on the broad brushstroke, except for Bensaúde painting[371].

Finally, at the plastic level and in order not to lengthen the analysis scope of this report too much, the threshold relation of the figure-bottom contour line appears in the works of Santos, Reis and Bensaúde is homogeneous, mixing the two pictorial masses in a kind of fog. However, in the works of Manta and Franco, the boundary line is well demarcated by a darker and stronger outline, delimiting the figure of the background in a clear and heterogeneous way.

---

[371] TABORDA, José da Cunha – Regras da arte da pintura: com breves reflexões críticas sobre os caracteres distintivos de suas escolas, vidas e quadros de seus mais célebres professores., p. 16.

Starting with a concrete analysis and collecting information from the canon - head / body relationship[372] – we can observe, using criteria addressed by Stratz that the paintings by Manta and Bensaúde were made with a proportion of 71/2 heads and two hypotheses can be raised. The first is the fact that both students and, more specifically, Abel Manta, since Bensaúde's life is unknown, have followed a more naturalistic canon.

The second hypothesis is based on the representation of Manta and Bensaúde based on an approximation to realism, with this naturalistic basis, which may indicate that the model would have an approximate height of 170 cm[373].

The painting by Santos e Reis, on the other hand, with a more elongated canon, on the one hand could indicate that both painters approach a more neo-classical current, or else that the model would have a height between 175-180 cm[374].

Finally, the canon represented by Franco, according to Straz's criteria, would represent a short man, with height between 165-170 cm[375]. However, looking closely at Franco's work, the representation of the total dimension of the leg is too

---

[372] Measurement values presented in the studies correspond to the dimension of the photograph and not to actual dimensions (without unit of measurement).

[373] STRATZ, C.H. – La figura humana en el arte. p. 9.

CLIMENT, op. cit., p. 7.

[374] STRATZ, op. cit., p. 9.

CLIMENT, op. cit., p. 7.

[375] Cf. LANGER, Carl – **Anatomie der äussen formen des menschlichen korpers**. Wien: Toeplitx & Deuticke, 1884.

RICHER, Paul – **Canon des proportions du corps humain**. Paris: Libraire Ch. Delagrave, 1893.

STRATZ, op. cit., p. 9.

CLIMENT, op. cit., p. 7.

short in relation to the rest of the body[376]. That is, the height of the pelvis corresponds approximately to the center of the total height of the model and in this case, the height of the lower half is less in relation to the upper half.

This representation may be associated with a high perspective that the painter would be in relation to the model, but not justified by the representation of the dimension of the lower limbs (feet) and his in relation to the head.

In this way, it is possible to raise some hypotheses of proportion representation of this contest, with the painting of Manta and Bensaúde being closer to its correct representation, gaining a lot in terms of shape, line, color, perspective and shadow the representation of Manta.

Curiously, in the eyes of José Augusto-França, Henrique Franco would have won the competition unfairly, the painter Abel Manta deserving of the chair.

> *Tal como Dordio, «moderno» para uns e «tradicionalista» para outros, e mais ainda do que ele, Manta sofreu ambas as classificações. Referindo-se às provas do concurso para professor das Belas-Artes, em 1934, o crítico d' O Diabo, interrogava polemicamente: «São estes os propulsores da ideia nova, do vanguardismo pictural? É melhor fechar a loja!»* [377] *. Dois anos depois, alguém apreciaria um tanto ingenuamente retratos de Manta: «Pintar como (ele) é ser moderno, é ser querido e sempre apreciado...».*[378]

With the brief analysis carried out, it is possible to agree with the statement by Augusto-França (at least at the anatomical

---

[376] Isto, tendo em conta que desconhecemos a verdadeira anatomia do modelo e mais nenhum pintor realizou esta relação de proporções.

[377] BRITO, Nogueira *in O Diabo* de 25 de novembro de 1934.

[378] FRANÇA, José-Augusto – A Arte em Portugal no século XX: 1911-1961. p. 123.

level). On the other hand, respecting the evaluation carried out in 1934, we can observe at the plastic level divergent aspects of each painter, being the most "impolite" of Franco and the most natural of Manta.

It is hoped through this chapter to demonstrate the importance of using the virtual to study academic paintings - PhD theme, as well as to find more documentation related to this competition. This is because, through the study of the proportion, we can observe several teaching schools and different theoretical bases.

Finally, it will be possible through this typology of pictorial analysis, consisting of the first step of studying the paintings, even if they will be studied analytically (methods of examination and analysis), remember that the document itself that represents the painting should never be discolored - painting itself.

Ramalho Ortigão

On February 8, 2015, Ramalho Ortigão (1836-1915) commemorated, with Raul Brandão (1867-1930), a great recognizer of his eclectic and hybrid work[379].

As an art critic in the 70s of the 19th century, Ramalho Ortigão was interested in the production of his time - the naturalism emerging after romanticism[380]. Naturalism emerged as a confrontation with romanticism and, in Portugal, through the plastic discussion between José Malhoa, Silva Porto, Columbano Bordalo Pinheiro, among others, who were the agitation of a new model of thought, in line with what was done in the rest from Europe.

The question of naturalism is important not only at the level of thought, but also at the level of the plastic arts, through Parisian influences and the plastic and stylistic ability. In this way, Ramalho Ortigão, referred to a huge void, where the artists were rebels and iconoclasts:

> De facto, existe uma tendência da história cultural portuguesa em privilegiar os anos de brasa, em que rebeldes e iconoclastas, neste particular, os jovens da geração de setenta, partiram a louça, a tranquilidade e a modorra da capital do país, a mais incaracterística e banal do mundo, segundo Ramalho Ortigão[381].

Ramalho becomes a defender of this new generation of neoclassicism, romanticism and naturalism than the "Generation

---

[379] 8 de fevereiro de 2015: Dia Ramalho Ortigão no CCB. See more at http://www.app.pt/6333/8-de-fevereiro-de-2015-dia-ramalho-ortigao-no-ccb/ [14-06-2015].

[380] MOOG – Eça de Queiroz e o século XIX. p. 153.

[381] ORTIGÃO – Eça de Queirós e Ramalho Ortigão: entre a Geração de Setenta e os Vencidos da Vida. p. 56.

of Seventy", worthy of the criticism incurred by a Ramalho Ortigão.

In this way, Ortigão became a mantle of this criticism, by locating and substantiating these young people in spite of tradition. On the other hand, Ortigão was a man who appreciated the art of his time, a defender of naturalism, a counterpart of the classic and the romantic. In addition, he also developed work in the area of Heritage, having been an important character in the rediscovery of Nuno Gonçalves' panels and in the defense of the Portuguese Primitives[382].

In this way, he was linked to the defense of heritage and interest in it, which revitalized his trips abroad, visiting countries such as France, England, Holland and even Brazil[383].

At this time, the idea of Positivism was developing, diminishing the importance of religious metaphysics, in which art could diminish this view through what it produced, replacing that same religious experience.

Ramalho Ortigão knows the international art of his time, not only interested in the major arts, such as plastic arts, but also in the minor arts. On the other hand, he was the promoter of the chronicle factory in Caldas da Rainha, supporting Rafael Bordalo Pinheiro a lot. On the other hand, it considered smaller arts, such as furniture, embroidery, tapestry, etc., of interesting to Ortigão as the major arts.

---

[382] ALVES – Ramalho Ortigão e o Culto dos Monumentos Nacionais no Século XIX. pp. 343-367.

[383] *Cf.* ZAN, João Carlos – Ramalho Ortigão e o Brasil. São Paulo: Faculdade de Filosofia, Letras e Ciências Humanas da Universidade de São Paulo, 2009. Tese de doutoramento em Letras, especialidade de Estudos Comparados de Literaturas de Língua Portuguesa.

CABETE, Susana Margarida – Le récir de voyage au Portugal au XIXème siècle: altérité et identité nationale. Paris: Université Paris III – Sorbonne Nouvelle. Thèse de Doctorat en Littérature Générale et Comparée.

Ramalho Ortigão wrote a lot for the newspapers and was interested in everything, being a humanist in the concept of Leonardo Da Vinci. If he had to choose an area to write, it would be that of the Arts, since he does not consider himself an art critic.

In his way of seeing the world, he had a vision more of our time and not so much of the late 19th century, being considered an author in the midst of writer and essayist.

"There was a panel in Ramalho's pen", stated Eça de Queiroz[384]. Ramalho belonged to the Generation of 70 and this group joined in the Cenacle[385], and later, they gave rise to the 90 Life Lords[386], of which Father Manuel Vieira and, later, Professor Manuel Antunes quotes: "at twenty we are arsonists and at fifty we are firefighters"[387].

Ramalho's description of the Cenacle, about the great figure of Antero de Quental, was given as the *irrequieto e carismático Antero de Quental [que] seduziu muitos jovens com uma impressionante oratória e a sua pena e tinteiro*[388]. The Vencidos da Vida action group is described as *que representa, no*

[385] *Cf.* SCHNERR – Ramalho Ortigão and the Generation of 1870. pp. 42-46.

ORTIGÃO – Eça de Queirós e Ramalho Ortigão: entre a Geração de Setenta e os Vencidos da Vida. pp. 56-61.

AA. VV. – **Os Vencidos da Vida: Ciclo de Conferências promovido pelo círculo de Eça de Queiroz.** Lisboa: C.E.Q., 1989, pp. 139-140.

[386] ORTIGÃO – Aurélia de Sousa em contexto: A cultura artística no fim de século. p. 111.

[387] ORTIGÃO – Eça de Queirós e Ramalho Ortigão: entre a Geração de Setenta e os Vencidos da Vida. pp. 56-61.

[388] SOÁREZ, Ednilo – Século XIX: um Portugal, duas literaturas, 2007, p. 24, texto Available at http://www.ceara.pro.br/acl/revistas/Colecao_Diversos/Literatura_Port_Brasil/ACL_LITE_POR_E_BR_2007_05_Seculo_XIX_um_Portugal_duas_literaturas_EDNILO_SOAREZ.pdf [09-04-2015].

desenrolar da história pátria, a mais fecunda e a mais pacífica das revoluções totais, levadas a cabo com uma elegância de atitudes que impressiona (...)[389].

The sculptor Célestin Anatole Calmels (1822-1906), decides to put himself in the shoes of a critic of naturalistic art, writing about a painting on which onions were represented. Camels, in a newspaper article, criticizes and censors the then painting of onions as "suitable for cooks", not knowing that the painter was Ramalho de Ortigão's own daughter. After Camels' criticism of his daughter, Ramalho will give rise to the letter from the 2nd Volume of Farpas, where he explains that he [Camels] is "an ignorant", signing with the pseudonym of "Simplício Feijão, the farmer", building from this way, the "art manifesto"[390]. For this purpose, he seeks paintings from the 17th century with ugly themes to defend his thesis, academic aesthetic theory, naturalistic perspective.

Ortigão also had the kinesthetic ability he was unaware of, seeing colors in the names of people, for example the name Luísa, which corresponds to the color blue. This psychological associative phenomenon has already been described by countless scholars in the field, and it is important to highlight the study by Francis Wood[391], André von Wattenwyl and Heinrich Zollinger [392].

Finally, a reference was made to Umberto Eco's anthropological metaphor, in its relationship between literature,

---

[389] AA. VV. – **Vencidos da Vida.** Ciclo de Conferências promovido pelo Século, Lisboa: Século, 1941, pp. V/VI

[390] *Cf.* QUEIRÓS, Eça de; ORTIGÃO, Ramalho – **As Farpas: Chronica Mensal da Política, das Letras e dos Costumes**. Lisboa: Emprenza Litteraria Luso-Brazileira, 1883.

[391] *Cf.* WOOD – The Origin of Color-Names. pp. 225-229.

[392] WATTENWYL; ZOLLINGER – Color-Term Salience and Neurophysiology of Color Vision. pp. 279-288.

social structure in semiotic terms[393] and also to the film *O Misterio da Estrada de Sintra*, based on the joint literary works of Eça de Queirós and Ramalho Ortigão[394].

---

[393] LEMERT – Language, Structure, and Measurement: Structuralist Semiotics and Sociology. pp. 929-957.

[394] *Cf.* QUEIRÓS, Eça de – **O mistério da estrada de Sintra**. Lisboa: Livros do Brasil, 197?.

Shadow Theater in India

In order to explore the notion of shadow, relating it to the metaphysical shadow archetype as an expression of religious thought, based on the famous epics of *Mahabharata* and *Ramayana*[395].

In the shadow theater there is a permanent relationship between image and text, the text having been only oral tradition, with a textual and figurative dimension in which it is often not possible to determine its antiquity, even though its form and materiality.

Shadow theater has its origins as an object in ancient times, from which it is not possible to confirm its birth precisely, but most academics geographically place its principle in Asia, namely in India, Indonesia, Central Asia and China[396].

The "Shadow Puppet" is a puppet related to painting and cultural tradition as an oral tradition. On the other hand, it is interesting the constant need for man to illustrate things, where ideas are converted into images, becoming illustrations. As an example, Christianity has been extensively illustrated since the 4th century AD, following the Codex[397]. This oral tradition of mythological narratives is permanently present in the religious passages that structure civilization.

---

[395] PASSOS – Esboço dum vocabulário aryano: *Vedas, Mahabarata* e *Ramayana*. pp. 20-23

[396] CHEN – Theaters of the World. pp. 25-64.

[397] *Cf.* KAZADOY – The Origin of Early Christian Book Illumination: The State of the Question. pp. 33-40.

These pictorial issues of shadow movements can be seen in the exhibition on the 2nd floor of the Oriente Foundation, in Lisbon[398].

In India, 6 styles are identified in different regions, making up the greatest influence of Southeast Asia, since all traditions in that region are adaptations of the themes of *Mahabharata* and *Ramayana*[399].

In these stories, the figure of the "Avatar" is descended (from God to become a body on earth) from the deities to the earth through the shadow theater[400], like, for example, the story of Krishna disappearing, giving rise to the 4th Age (the present).

In fact, it is religious stories that pass moral and ethical stories, with resonance of archetypes in the emanation of these bodies - what does the shadow mean to man? And why is this shadow?

The relationship between shadow and painting, originating from the shadow archetype, can be approached based on the analytical psychology of Carl Jung (1875-1961), founder of the archetypes[401]. According to this author, the shadow is a projection of the ego (me), that is, a projection of what is our subconscious[402].

---

[398] See more at http://www.foriente.pt/ [16-06-2015].

[399] CHEN, op. cit., p. 33.

BLACKBURN, Stuart – **Inside the Drama-House: Rama Stories and Shadow Puppets in South India**. California: University of California Press, 1996.

[400] LYALL – Brahmanisn. pp. 920-934.

[401] *Cf.* JUNG, Carl – **The red book**. New York: W. W. Norton & Company, 2009.

Idem – **Tipos psicológicos**. Rio de Janeiro: Zahar, 1974.

[402] *Cf.* COWARD, Harold – Taoism and Jung: Synchronicity and the Self. Philosophy East and West, Vol. 46, n.º 4 (1996), pp. 477-495.

In Jung's perspective, it is the projection of the repression of light and what is projected in the shadow, is the dark side of people, corresponding only to bad things. However, this theory can be criticized because we also project expectations and good things. In this way, the shadow archetype goes beyond the projection of the self, transcending it.

On the other hand, the positive projection of the shadow can be given with the example of the Bible - Psalms, Chap. 17, in verses 8 and 9, in which God protects humanity through his "wings": "(8) Protects me as the apple of your eyes; / hide me in the shadow of your wings, / (9) the wicked who attack me with violence, / the mortal enemies that surround me. "[403]

The positive shadow has a tradition in Hinduism, in which many of the deities are represented as shadowy figures (not necessarily negative, even negative with positivity). These shadows are aggressive and act as a deterrent to evil, as referred to in the epic *Shilappadikaram*: "The puppets danced with war-like vigor just as goddess *Lakshmi* danced to destroy the *Rashasas* (demons)"[404]. In this case, the red of fury turns into positive destruction, eliminating those who do evil, in order to appeal to justice in humanity (divine fury).

On the other hand, the shadow itself is a reflection of the virtues that serve as an example and the bodies of spirits and individuals, are dualism of presence and physical absence. Angels and divine figures intervene even though we cannot see them. Thus, the same happens with the shadow and, even more so, in the shadow theater, this representation is a shadow of that shadow itself (duality).

In material terms, these objects have varying thicknesses, which allow the light to pass through and observe the colors. These figures can be made in black and white or in color, and the

---

[403] http://www.bibliaon.com/salmos_17/ [01-04-2015].
[404] GHOSH; BANERJEE – Indian puppets. p. 15.

positive figures are made from deer skin or other, resulting from noble hunting. The other lower figures are made from pig and buffalo skin, corresponding to less noble fighters[405]. On the other hand, they are also composed of different opacities and the divine figures are stored separately from the other figures[406].

In the process of building these shadows, the last parts to apply color are the eyes, constituting that moment as the passage of the manifestation of the God who is represented. In this case, we have a duality of presence through colors, absence, shadow and invocation of the Gods who are invited to incorporate the object.

The divine presence at the time of the theater is essential and composes the latent idea of treating the traditional puppet like blessed gods, showing dignity and respect[407]. On the other hand, there is a religious character in the sense that it will bring goods to the families that order them. In this way, the bodies of the deities have shadow quality through the virtues that define that same deity.

Still, shade in India has an impact across castes. The importance attached to the shadow corresponds to integrity, being affected by something that inflates the person's character and Karma. That is, lower castes need to be careful that their physical shadow is not projected on the shadow of people of higher castes, raising questions at the moral and ethical level. This shadow is double of the "I", giving as an example if someone hurts another's shadow, that person would suffer and feel that pain at the physical level, that is, the shadow is extremely important and has a double physical nature.

In fact, the shadow is interconnected with the birth of painting and, particularly in Europe, in Book X of the *Republic* of

---

[405] Idem, p. 25.

[406] Idem, p. 54.

[407] Idem, p. 22.

Plato[408]. We also find in the work of Pliny, 35, Chap. 43, the birth of painting, with Carinthia, projecting and drawing the profile from the shadow of her husband. Once but, the representation (of the portrait) is made from the shadow[409].

On the other hand, in Plato's Allegory of the Cave, we have one of the first examples of the shadow theater, where puppets of men and animals would apparently be manipulated behind these men of the "audience"[410].

Another example, the myth in which family members asked the God of Death for a deceased through his portrait, bringing the relative back to earth. Another myth describes a sober man in the countryside who lets muses approach with the idea of seducing him. To resist, from their shadow, she draws a stunning female figure, instilling life in her, making the others embarrassed by her beauty and withdraw.

In fact, we know the shadow theater from the storytellers, who at some point felt the need to illustrate them, using fire to illuminate and represent them through painting.

The figures used in the shadow theater can be various characteristics, for example, the almond and loaded eyes (Pinguli), are recurrent in these figures, influenced by the Islamic invasion of the 7th century, a century after the introduction of the shadow theater in India[411]. In the shadow theater, they use

---

[408] *Cf.* PLATÃO – **A República**. Lisboa: Fundação Calouste Gulbenkian, 1983.

[409] See more at
http://www.perseus.tufts.edu/hopper/text?doc=Perseus%3Atext%3A1
999.02.0137%3
Abook%3D35%3Achapter%3D43 [16-06-2015].

[410] CHEN, op. cit., pp. 25-64.

QUIRINO – Sombra – do Vestígio ao Enigma. p. 7.

[411] CHEN, op. cit., p. 32.

GHANI – The Study of Semiotics Wayang Kulit Theatre in Malay Culture Society. pp. 321-335.

the same codes for the figures, based on the painting treatises, which try to regulate the practice, incorporating mural painting, folio and shadow theater. Taking as an example, the color code, in which the bluish figures correspond to purity, women are portrayed through pale yellow, the demons in red, etc., that is, there are recipes for using colors.

Even so, these rules are not strict, so much so that art treatises include performance and can indicate dramatic notions of colors, such as white for the representation of joy, gray for the pathetic, red for the beautiful, etc.

Francisco de Holanda

Although it was only in the mid-18th century that theories of genius were philosophically systematized, we already have some ideas in the 15th century, such as the rise of the Craftsman to Genius, as a Man to Divine[412], developed by Francisco de Holanda (1517-1585). Francisco de Holanda developed several theses, such as *Da Pintura Antiga* (original from 1548)[413] and *Diálogos em Roma*[414].

In fact, at the time of Francisco de Holanda, there was no word "artist" and even Vasari indicated artists as artisans[415]. In Portugal, this issue took a long time to have this conversion and even to instill and dignify the artist's theory.

In this way, the Netherlands had a great boldness, fueled by their contacts in Évora that allowed them to articulate new ideas and, in this way,, prepare for their trip to Italy, where they contacted with the high renaissance[416]. Em Roma, fascina-se com tudo e especialmente com a figura de Miguel Ângelo.

1. Metaphysics of God's Creation and Imitation, from which Ancient Painting begins; 2. Idea; 3. Characterization of the painter; 4. Exceptionality; 5. Melancholy; 6. Innate talent. Holanda defended the idea of artist as a genius (originality), with

---

[412] LOUSÃ – A defesa do estatuto do artista na obra de Francisco de Holanda. 94-105.

[413] *Cf.* HOLANDA, Francisco de – **Da Pintura Antiga**. Lisboa: Imprensa Nacional-Casa da Moeda, 1986.

[414] *Cf.* HOLANDA, Francisco de – **Diálogos em Roma**. Lisboa: Livros Horizonte, 1984.

[415] *Cf.* VASARI, Giorgio – **Le vite de' piú eccellenti pittori, scultori e architettori**. Novara: Istituto Geografico de Agostini, 1967.

[416] *Cf.* VILELA, José Stichini – **Francisco de Holanda: vida, pensamento e obra.** Lisboa: Instituto de Cultura e Língua Portuguesa, 1982.

connections to Kant, Hegel and Schopenhauer, with the following aesthetic foundations presented by the speaker: 1. From the metaphysics of creation to the Painter as "Deus in terris"; 2. The idea or invention; 3. Furor Divinus.

On the first point, the way he describes the origin of the painting, is framed in a context and trend of the time, following the classics, as Aristotle also begins his written works through causes. Thus, Holanda also begins his writing in Da Pintura Antiga, by enunciating the causes that led him to carry out this written work.

In this work, the invocation is the idea of "God painter", since there was already the God sculptor who made Adam out of clay and thus Holland had the audacity to bring the God painter. Thus, he developed the concept of "God was a painter", attributing the origin of painting to a divine cause and where you can find the paraphrase of painting that Holland adds to his aesthetic theory [417].

For this author, painting is associated with divine genesis, its origin coinciding with the origin of the world. In fact, he uses Demiúrgica for greater legitimation of painting and painter. Thus, God-Painter is placed in the center, the painter being an imitator of the divine will and creation with a special mission of a demiurgical character.

> *Da fonte da pintura e primeira causa será o começo de nossa obra; onde podemos dizer ser Deos pintor evidentissimo, e nas suas obras se conteer todo o exemplo e sustancia de tal arte. Portque de duas cousas a pintura é formada, sem as quaes não se poderia pintar alguma obra: a primeira é a lux ou claro, a segunda he escuro ou sombra, e como deixa de ser sombra, logo vem o claro, e no fim do claro começa a sombra; as quaes duas colores acordadas em sua deminuição ou crecimento pintarão todas as cousas.*

---

[417] HOLANDA – Da Pintura Antiga. p. 24.

*Deos quando quiz pintar tudo o que vemos, como
perfectissimo pintor, sobre a escuridade e treuas que cobria
o grão retauolo do mundo, começou logo com o claro, e por
isto he mas nobre o claro que o escuro: que foi a primeira
mão de Deus; e a boa pintura com claro se deue começar
sobre o escuro e não com escuro como todos fazem.[418]*

Interestingly, for Holland the light is more noble than the
dark, representing light and shadow as two primary elements of
divine process. In this way, everything develops through its
creation, light and shadow are responsible for the creation of
time.

On the other hand, the valorization of chiaroscuro, due to
medieval influence, defends the application of light and even for
Saint Augustine, defender of light, one should start with light and
not with shadow. However, it can also consist of Platonic
metaphysics, in the sense that light is the representation of the
soul at that time and the irrational, of the shadow. At this point,
we can relate these issues directly to the theme addressed in the
previous subchapter, referring to the Shadow Theater.

More than painting being creation, it is creation being
painting, under Platonic influence, the trip to Italy being a
landmark of Holland's intellectual life and the main theoretical
influence being Plato (428-348? BC). For Plato, when dealing
with issues related to creation, poetry is referred to, this concept
being described as the ability to pass non-being into being, just
as the painter God did in Holland[419].

The *Idades do Mundo* by Holanda[420], it presents itself as
an illustrated bible, with the 6 ages of the world in accordance

[418] Idem, pp. 21/22.

[419] PLATÃO – **O Banquete**. Lisboa: Edições 70, 1991.

[420] *Cf.* DESWARTE-ROSA, Sylvie; CHICÓ, Maria Alice – **As Imagens das
Idades do Mundo de Francisco de Holanda**. Lisboa: Imprensa
Nacional-Casa da Moeda, 1987.

with Iberian script and iconography. This work by Holanda starts with representation through color until mortal sin, and is presented in black and white until the resurrection of Christ, being represented again through color from that moment on.

Just as God painted the past with light, charged with a Neoplatonic symbolic charge, this is the original one due to the absence of the bearded man and other anthropomorphic representations. Thus, the metaphysics of creation is light as a demiurgical (divine) source.

The image's answer for Holland is God, the original, in relation to everything that was expected, without anthropomorphic representation and, consequently, without the bearded man.

Thus, Holland establishes that the mastery of painting is divine and human. The first, divine because it creates and animates (inflates) and the second because of its unconscious character. Still, Holanda notes that the imitation performed is not of nature, but of God's divine activity (unlike Leon Battista Alberti (1404-1472) in his relationship with nature)[421].

In this way, the painter is "God on Earth", via ideas or *cosa mentale* and painting is a statement of thought, as for Da Vinci, the same concept of *cosa mentale.*

> *Mostremos primeiramente que cousa he esta ciencia de que queremos tratar para sermos melhor entendidos e digamos que cousa e a pintura, quanto ao que d'ella entendemos. A pintura diria eu que era uma declaração de pensamento em obra vesivil e contemplatiua, e segundo natureza.*[422]

---

[421] *Cf.* AFONSO, Nuno – <u>Pintura antiga como Prisca Theologia: Francisco de Holanda e a tradição hermética</u>. Lisboa: Faculdade de Belas-Artes da Universidade de Lisboa, 2001. Tese de Mestrado em Teoria da Arte.

[422] HOLANDA – Da Pintura Antiga. p. 26.

Holland also addresses the imitation of God's activity, where painting becomes the action of creating again, while divine or natural works and its painting imitates the divine, approaching what is divine. Like God, the artist creates again, on a smooth and clean board, looking somewhere for what he produces and creates[423].

> E é finalmente a pintura fazer e criar de nouo numa tauoa limpa e lisa, ou num papel cego e inobre, criar e fazer de nuou quesquer obras, divinas ou naturaes, com tão perfeita emitação.[424]

In this way, Holanda never forgets that correlation between the Divine and the Human, where the Divine is earlier, despite its structural and metaphysical dependence.

On the other hand, a key part of Holland's philosophy is to dignify artistic activity. It demonstrates that the arts are also science and formed by 3 precepts: Idea, Proportion, Decorum or Decency. First, the Idea is central and any artifice in the drawing needs proportion, and decency has to do with the good sense of the story to be represented, it has to do with the content.

An example of Decorum or Decency is the image of Pietà by Miguel Ângelo (1475-1564) of the Virgin with Jesus, where the Virgin appears to be 18 years old and Jesus at 33 years old, is not decorum.

The Idea, as referred to by the Netherlands, is an "invention" and constitutes an important milestone for the initiation of this theme and its relationship with artistic creation. In this way, Holanda begins his explanation of the creative process with the determination that "imagination will make the idea", accentuating and determining the fantasy, from which

[423] LOUSÃ – O pintor como Deus in Terris: de Ficino a Francisco de Holanda. pp. 23-30.
[424] HOLANDA – Da Pintura Antiga. p. 28.

Decorum arises in relation to the theme that it is intended to represent.

For Holland, fantasy and imagination are equivalent to understanding, trying to differentiate that the artist's work is not merely intellectual, but resulting from the activity of the intellect. In this case, Holland has as sources Vitruvius (1st century BC) and Giorgio Vasari (1511-1574) who also use this terminology[425].

The painter grants the Idea with care and Decency, the idea appears as illumination but it is necessary to meditate, linked to the selection of the idea that he had, and should take a while to make Holland never say that it is the product of mimesis or imitation of nature[426]. In this way, the meditation process is reflection and it becomes more important to know what you do not want to paint, and the importance of the selection process arises.

> Mas se o valente homem veo a fazer uma obra que todos louvão por stremada e a elle mesmo o parece; e todavia não é a que elle tinha imaginado na sua idea, nem a que elle desejou que viesse a ser; não se deve por isso de ter por contente; antes a tal obra deve de desmanchar e destruir, e comece de novo as vias com que venha a ser com os olhos carnaes o que ve com os do sprito.[427]

The idea is invisible, from thought, but when it has resolved enlightenment and meditation, then most of the work is done and between proportion and decorum.

In the artistic mind, thinking with images is more present and the faculty of the Idea is imagination, as an imagistic understanding. For Saint Augustine (354-430), it is the definition

---

[425] *Cf.* DESWARTE, Sylvie – **Ideias e imagens em Portugal na época dos descobrimentos: Francisco de Holanda e a teoria da arte.** Lisboa: Difel, 1992.

[426] HOLLANDA – A ideia na Pintura. pp. 56/57.

[427] HOLANDA – Da Pintura Antiga. pp. 93/94.

of "inner eyes", where the inner world is processed, but as a connection to the divine and the spirit, without irrational character.

In this way, imagination is a faculty of ideas, where the work of art is done when the painter already has an image in thought - connection with the conceptual. Thus, Holanda resorts to the definition of Platonic idea, although it is referring to particular and not universal ideas when referring to the painter's ideas.

Plato will say that we were born with ideas and over time, we will remember, but for Holland, each idea is the creation of a work of art, being a product of contemplation before practice and, in this way, represents a connection to the divine.

Only when the painter changes to proportion and decorum does he become sensitive. Thus, Holanda values and emphasizes the intellectual aspect of painting and goes further, taking into account the artist's imagination. Thus, it considers artistic freedom, not going to meet the renaissance, but rather the mannerism (maniera).

On the other hand, it is also possible to see in the painter's praise a kind of defense in relation to Platonic criticism in book X da *República*, in which the arts are not part of the ideal society[428]. For Holanda, art is not simulacrum because it copies from the cosa mentale and not from the empirical world, having as its influence the figure of Miguel Ângelo, regarding the *Diálogos em Roma*.

For Holland, God would have had ideas before making the world, thus dividing into macrocosms what reports to God and microcosms to the painter. On the other hand, the expression

---

[428] *Cf.* PLATÃO – **A República**. Lisboa: Fundação Calouste Gulbenkian, 1983.

that was used in the fashion of *Furor Divinus*, was understood as the inspiration that the painter instilled in his production.

> *[...] e se ser podesse pôr-se com stylo na mão e faze-la com os olhos tapados, melhor seria, por não perder aquele divino furor e imagem que na fantesia leva.*[429]

On the other hand, sketchy is the sketch, the first register of the idea, something quick not to forget, the expression with closed eyes stands out, recording only your imagination, citing the imitation of the sensitive world. This concept was recovered from Plato - from the madness and inspiration of the masses in his works *Íon*[430] and *Fédon*[431] – state of divine possession and considered the inspiration (poets). In this way, possessed by magnetic forces - muses - resulting in productive madness, in which the poet is divine or human, but is not the creator of his knowledge.

Thus, the artist's intellect is valued, under the influence of the Council of Trent (1545-1563), in which the divine Furor the connection with God. On the other hand, the idea of "blind eyes" is medieval, with the valorization of irrational forces and the unconscious being innovative for the time. However, Marsilio Ficino (1433-1499) had also already done so, but only for poets (influence of Plato), priests and saints.

The theme of the characterization of the painter as a genius is presented in his work Da Pintura Antiga, where he carries out the psychological characterization of the painter, becoming an original subject.

On the question "How should the painter be?", Holanda hesitantly describes the psychological nature and exceptional personality as worthy of freedom. Namely in the works

---

[429] HOLANDA – Da Pintura Antiga. p. 93.

[430] *Cf.* PLATÃO – **Íon**. Lisboa: Inquérito, 2000.

[431] *Cf.* PLATÃO – **Fédon: Diálogo sobre a imortalidade da alma.** Coimbra: Atlântida, 1947.

Dialogues in Rome and Ancient Painting, he complains about emotions and life, bringing aspects of his own personality.

Thus, Holanda defends the idea that the true artist has no choice and, consequently, he has to accept what he has to do, carrying a missionary load of his talent from the divine charge of the painter God. Still, he argues that artistic talent is born with the individual and even affirms issues of heredity.

> *N'isso sonhará, n'isso vegiará, n'isso porá todo seu gosto e felicidade, sem nunca antepôr nenhum desgosto nem incomodo dos em que continuamente vê viver os outros inorantes pintores. E atentando bem n'isso achará não serem aquelles os que elle deseja de ser e emitar, e seguirá contente e cegamente só o divino nome na pintura com os grandes stimolos que lhe pedirá seu natural engenho e tudo o outro terá por vil e por baxeza senão sómente a vertude que lhe seu pensamento e spirito desejam.[432]*

The painter does not imitate what is done, but it is original and this theory was innovative at the time. On the other hand, it justifies the artist's truth and the fact that he is not melancholy, since the painting is intellectual, requires time and little social life. Nevertheless, Holanda describes the painter's profile as rebellious by nature, not being concerned with social appearances.

The theme of "Pintor como Génio" has direct links with the theses defended by Kant in his Critical work at Faculdade do Juízo, namely from §46 to 49. In this work, the notion of "genius" consists of an 18th century theory, with an approach that brings meaning to the whole work.

For Kant, genius is limited to the field of the arts and only the artist, since, using Newton and other scientists as an example, they are able to use the scientific method to explain how they arrive at a certain idea.

---

[432] HOLANDA – Da Pintura Antiga. p. 56.

In the case of Holanda and the question of Divine Furor, the artist does not know how to explain certain ideas and in this case, the talent is innate, productive, non-contemplative and gifted by God. Thus, the artist is chosen, rare and exceptional.

Referências

A

AA. VV. – Vencidos da Vida. Ciclo de Conferências promovido pelo Século, Lisboa: Século, 1941, pp. V/VI

AA. VV. – **La pintura al temple, Introducción general al arte**. Madrid: Ed. Istmo, 1980.

AA. VV. – Os Vencidos da Vida: Ciclo de Conferências promovido pelo círculo de Eça de Queiroz. Lisboa: C.E.Q., 1989, pp. 139-140.

AA.VV. – **A permanência do corpo: academias da escola de Lisboa**. Lisboa: Reitoria da Universidade de Lisboa, 1999.

AA. VV., *The Impressionists Handbook: The Great Works and the World That Inspired Them*, Metro books, New York, 2000.

AA. VV. – **Casa de Santa Maria em Cascais: Raul Lino**. Cascais: Câmara Municipal, 2005.

AA.VV. – **Figures du corps : Une leçon d'anatomie à l'école des Beaux-Arts**. Paris: ENSBA – École des Beaux Arts de Paris, 2008.

AA. VV. – **Primitivos Portugueses 1450 -1550, O Século de Nuno Gonçalves**. Lisboa: Athena, 2011.

AA. VV. – **Colóquio Nacional Raul Lino em Sintra, Casa dos Penedos**. Actas do II Ciclo de Conferências, coord. Rodrigo Sobral Cunha, 25 e 26 de Junho de 2004. Sintra: Castelo do Amor, 2014.

AA.VV., Os últimos dias: desenhos de Alexandre Conefrey, Paulo Brighenti, Rui Moreira, Rui Vasconcelos, Lisboa, Centro de Arte Moderna José De Azeredo Perdigão, 2000.

ADAMS, Laurie, The Methodologies of Art, an introduction, New York, Icon Editions, 1996.

ADOLPHS, Ralph, Recognizing Emotion From Facial Expressions: Psychological and Neurological Mechanisms, University of Iowa College of Medicine, 2002.

ADORNO, Theodor W. – **Teoria estética**. Lisboa: Edições 70, 1993.

AFONSO, Nuno – Pintura antiga como Prisca Theologia: Francisco de Holanda e a tradição hermética. Lisboa: Faculdade de Belas-

Artes da Universidade de Lisboa, 2001. Tese de Mestrado em Teoria da Arte.

AIKEN, Edward – The Cinema and Italian Futurist Painting. Art Journal. Vol. 41, No. 4, 1981, pp. 353-357.

AGUIAR, Maria, *Os materiais e a técnica de pintura a óleo na obra de Aurélia de Souza e a sua relação com a conservação*, Tese de doutoramento em Conservação e Restauro, Universidade Católica do Porto, Porto, 2012.

ALANEN, Lilli, 'What Are Emotions about?', in Philosophy and Phenomenological Research, Volume 67, Number 2, 2003, pp. 311-334.

ALDEMIRA, Varela – A Pintura na teoria e na prática. Lisboa: Sociedade Industrial de Tipografia, 1969, p. 11.

ALMEIDA, Betâmio de, 'Ensino das Artes Plásticas', in Dicionário de História de Portugal, Volume II, Porto, Livraria Figueirinhas, 1999.

ALMEIDA, Pedro Vieira de – Raul Lino, Arquitecto Moderno. Raul Lino – Exposição Retrospectiva da sua Obra. Lisboa: Fundação Calouste Gulbenkian (1970), pp. 115-188.

ALMEIDA-MATOS, Lúcia, (coord.) *Desenhos do século XIX. O Museu Faculdade de Belas Artes da Universidade do Porto*, Porto, Faculdade de Belas-Artes da Universidade do Porto, 2000.

ALVES, Alice Nogueira – Ramalho Ortigão e o Culto dos Monumentos Nacionais no Século XIX. Lisboa: Faculdade de Letras da Universidade de Lisboa, 2009, pp. 343-367. Tese de doutoramento em História, especialidade de Arte, Património e Restauro.

ANDRADE, E.N., 'Galileo', in Notes and Records of the Royal Society of London, Volume 19, Number 2, 1964, pp. 120-130.

ANTUNES, João Lobo – **Anatomia: arte e ciência**. Lisboa: fundação Champalimaud, 2013.

APOSTOLIDÈS, Jean-Marie – Du Surréalism à l'Internationale situationniste: la question de l'image. MLN. Vol. 105, No. 4 (1990), pp. 727-749.

APTER, Michael J. – Cybernetics and Art. Leornardo. Vol. 2, No. 3 (1969), pp. 257-265.

ARAÚJO, Saulo, Artífice ou artista?: Uma problemática que acompanha o ensino superior em Portugal no século XIX, Dissertação de Mestrado em Teorias da Arte, Faculdade de Belas-Artes da Universidade de Lisboa, Lisboa, 2002.

ARGAN, Giulio Carlo, Guia de história da arte, Lisboa, Editorial Estampa, 1992.

ARISTÓTELES, Poética, Lisboa, Fundação Calouste Gulbenkian, 2004.

ASCOTT, Roy – Towards a Field Theory for Post-Modernist Art. Leonardo. Vol. 13, No. 1 (1980), pp. 51-52.

ASPEREN DE BOER, J.R.J. – Infrared reflectography: A method for the examination of paintings. Applied Optics,. Vol. 7, n° 1 (1968), pp. 1711–1714.

B

BARASCH, Moshe, 'The Crying Face', in Artibus et Historiae, Volume 8, Number 15, 1987, pp. 21-36.

BARCSAY, Jenö – **Anatomía artística del cuerpo humano**. Barcelona: Idea Books, D. L., 1996.

BARBARO, Daniel, *La Pratica della perspettiva*, [s.n.], C. et R. Borgominieri fratelli, 1568.

BARREIRA, João, Arte portuguesa, Lisboa, Edições Excelsior, [s.d.].

BARRETT, Estelle & BOLT, Barbara, *Practice as Research: Approaches to Creative Arts Enquiry*, London, I.B. Tauris & Co Ltd., 2010.

BARTRINA, Luís Villanueva, Perspectiva lineal, Su Construcción y su Relación con la Fotografia, Barcelona, Edicions UPC, 1996.

BAUDRILLARD, Jean – **De la Séduction**. Paris: Galilée, 1979.

BATAILLE, George et al., 'Dust', in *Encyclopaedia Acephalica (Atlas Arkhive)*, London, Atlas Press, pp. 42/43.

BAUMGARTEN, Alexander, Esthétique: précédée des Méditations philosophiques sur quelques sujets se rapportant à l'essence du poèm et de la métaphysique, Paris, L'Herne, 1988.

BAYER, Raymond, História da Estética, Lisboa, Estampa, 1995.

BERNARDO, José Viriato – A coleção de escultura da Faculdade de Belas Artes: a formação do gosto e o ensino do desenho. Lisboa: Faculdade de Belas-Artes de Lisboa, 2014, 2 vols. Tese de doutoramento em Belas-Artes, especialidade de Desenho.

BIRRINGER, Johannes – Performance and Science. A Journal of Performance and Art. Vol. 29, No. 1 (2007), pp. 22-35.

BIGGS, Michael, KARLSSON, Henrik, *The Routledge Companion to Research in the Arts (Routledge Companions)*, London, Routledge, 2012.

BLANC, Yves & DIMANICO, Ugo, 'History of the Study of Skeletal Muscle Function with Emphasis on Kinesiological Electromyography', in The Open Rehabilitation Journal, Volume 3, 2010, pp. 84-93.

BOLTER, Jay David – The Computer, Hypertext, and Classical Studies. The American Journal of Philology. Vol. 112, No. 4 (1991), pp. 541-545.

BORGDORFF, Henk, *The Conflict of the Faculties: Perspectives on Artistic Research and Academia*, Leiden, Leiden University Press, 2012.

BOSE, Phanindra Nath – Principles of Indian silpasastra with the text of Mayasastra. Varanasi: Bharatiya Pub. House, 1978.

BOUWSMA, O.K. – Descartes' Evil Genius. The Philosophical Review. Vol. 58, n° 2 (1949), pp. 141-151.

BLACKBURN, Stuart – Inside the Drama-House: Rama Stories and Shadow Puppets in South India. California: University of California Press, 1996.

BRIGHENTI, Paulo, Paulo Brighenti, Rui Vasconcelos: uma jornada, Funchal, Galeria porta 33, 2001.

BRITO, Nogueira de *in O Diabo* de 25 de novembro de 1934.

BRUNT, P. A., 'Marcus Aurelius in His Meditations', in The Journal of Roman Studies, Volume 64, 1974, pp. 1-20

BURGESS, Craig, 'Kant's Key to the Critique of Taste', in The Philosophical Quarterly, Volume 39, Number 157, 1989, pp. 484-192.

C

CABETE, Susana Margarida – Le récir de voyage au Portugal au XIXème siècle: altérité et identité nationale. Paris: Université Paris III – Sorbonne Nouvelle. Thèse de Doctorat en Littérature Générale et Comparée.

CAETANO, Joaquim Oliveira, 'Gregório Lopes – Pintor Régio e Cavaleiro de Santiago' in *As Ordens Militares em Portugal e no Sul da Europa*, Atas do II Encontro sobre Ordens Militares, Lisboa, Edições Colibri / Câmara Municipal de Palmela, 1997.

CALADO, Margarida, 'Desenhar o corpo – uma metodologia de ensino constante na arte ocidental', in *Representações do corpo na ciência e na arte*, Lisboa, 2012, pp. 109-124.

Idem, 'Ensino', in *Dicionário de Art Barroca*, (Dir.) PEREIRA, José Fernandes, Lisboa, Editorial Presença, 1989, pp. 160-163.

Idem, 'Academia do Nu', In PEREIRA, José Fernandes (Ed.) Dicionário da Arte Barroca em Portugal, Lisboa, Editorial Presença, 1989.

Idem, 'Ensino', In PEREIRA, José Fernandes (Ed.) Dicionário da Arte Barroca em Portugal, Lisboa, Editorial Presença,1989.

Idem, O Convento de S. Francisco da Cidade. Subsídios para uma Monografia, Lisboa, Faculdade de Belas-Artes da Universidade de Lisboa, 2011.

Idem, 'Desenhar o corpo - uma metodologia de ensino constante na arte ocidental', In TAVARES, Cristina Azevedo (Ed.) Representações do corpo na ciência e na arte, Fim de Século, Lisboa, 2011, pp. 109-124.

CALADO, Margarida & FERRÃO, Hugo, 'Da Academia à Faculdade de Belas-Artes', in *A Universidade de Lisboa nos séculos XIX-XX*, Lisboa, Universidade de Lisboa, Volume 2, pp. 1107-1151.CALADO, Maria Marques & CALADO, Maria Margarida, Desenhos dos Séculos XIX e XX - Escola Superior de Belas-Artes de Lisboa, Lisboa, Escola Superior de Belas Artes de Lisboa, 1975.

CALVO, Manuel G. & FERNÁNDEZ-MARTÍN, Andrés, 'Can the eyes reveal a person's emotions? Biasing role of the mouth expression', in Motivation and Emotion, DOI 10.1007/s11031-012-9298-1.

CÂMARA MUNICIPAL DO FUNCHAL – **Museu Henrique e Francisco Franco**. Funchal: Câmara Municipal do Funchal, 1987.

CAMPOS, Marta Gonçalves, *The Study of Lead White Oil Paints*, Dissertação de Mestrado em Conservação e Restauro, Faculdade de Ciência e Tecnologias da Universidade Nova de Lisboa, Monte de Caparica, 2010.

CARDEIRA, Ana Mafalda, *Caracterização material e técnica de 12 pinturas de académia de nu de José Veloso Salgado, pertencentes à coleção da FBAUL*, Dissertação de Mestrado em Ciências da Conservação, Restauro e Produção de Arte Contemporânea, Faculdade de Belas-Artes da Universidade de Lisboa, Lisboa, 2014.

CARDEIRA, Ana Mafalda, LONGELIN, Stéphane, COSTA, Sónia, CANDEIAS, António, CARVALHO, Maria Luísa & MANSO, Marta, 'Multi-analytical characterisation of D'Aprés Cormon by José Veloso Salgado', in Nuclear Instruments and Methods in Physics Research Section B: Beam Interactions with Materials and Atoms, Volume 331, pp. 271-274.

CARDEIRA, Ana Mafalda; LONGELIN, Stéphane; LE GAC, Agnés; NOGUEIRA, Isabel; CARVALHO, Maria Luísa; MANSO, Marta – Spectroscopic characterizatio of a contemporary Indian miniature painting. Applied Spectroscopy. Vol. 67, Issue 12 (2013), pp. 1376-1381.

CARDEIRA, Ana Mafalda; LONGELIN, Stéphane; COSTA, Sónia – Caracterização material e técnica da pintura de Veloso Salgado – contributo museológico. VOX MUSEI, Vol. 1, nº 1 (2013), pp. 64-72.

CARRIER-REYNAUD, Brgitte, *Enseignement professionnel et la formation technique (du XIXe siècle)*, Saint-Étienne, Publications de l'Université de Saint-Étienne, 2006.

CASALI, Franco – X-Ray Digital Radiography and Computed Tomography for Cultural Heritage. Archeometriai Mühely. Vol. 1, nº 1 (2006), pp. 24-28.

CERONI, Vittori – When Future Met Its Past (The "Futurism" of Filippo T. Marinetti). The Modern Language Journal. Vol. 28, No. 8 (1944), pp. 665-673.

CASIMIRO, Luís Alberto, 'Pintura e Escultura do Renascimento no Norte de Portugal', in *Ciências e Técnicas do Património*, Revista da Faculdade de Letras na Universidade do Porto, 2006-2007, I Série, Volume V-VI, pp. 87-114.

CASTRO, Machado de, *Discurso sobre as utilidades do desenho, dedicado à Rainha N. Senhora*, Lisboa, Offic. Da Academia das Sciencias, 1818.

CASTRO, Machado, *Dicionário de escultura*, Lisboa, Livraria Coelho, 1937.

CHAMULEAU, Jean Luc, As teorias da arte: filosofia, crítica e história da arte: de Platão aos nossos dias, Lisboa, Instituto Piaget, 1997.

CHAPIRO, Meyer, 'Style', in Anthropology Today: An Encyclopedia Inventory, Ed. KRÖBER, A. L., Chicago, University of Chicago Press, 1953, pp. 287-312.

CHASTEL, André, 'O Artista' in *O Homem Renascentista*, Lisboa, Presença, 1991.

CHEN, Fan Pen – Theaters of the World. Asian Folklore Studies. Vol. 62, n.º 1 (2003), pp. 25-64.

CHICÓ, Mário Tavares, Dicionário da Pintura Universal, 3 Volumes, Lisboa, Estúdios Cor, 1973.

CLARK, Bradford – A Celebration of Indian Puppetry. Asian Theatre Journal. Vol. 22, n.º 2 (2005), pp. 334-347.

CLIMENT, Carlos Plasencia; LANCE, Manuel Martínez – **Las proporciones humanas y los cánones artísticos**. Valencia: Editorial Universidad Politécnica de Valencia, 2007.

COESSENS, Katheleen, *The artistic turn: A Manifesto (Orphues Research Centre in Music Series ORCiM)*, Leuven, Leuven University Press, 2009.

COOK, Richard, BIRD, Geoffrey, CATMUR, Caroline, PRESS, Clare & HEYES, Cecilia, 'Mirror neurons: From origin to function', in The Behavioral and Brain Sciences, Volume 37, 2014, pp. 177-241.

CORREIA, Virgílio, Pintores portugueses dos séculos XV e XVI, Coimbra, Imprensa da Universidade, 1928.

COSTA, Félix, *The antiquity of the art of painting*, New Haven, Yale University, 1967.

COSTA, Luiz Xavier, *Ensino das Belas Artes nas obras do Real Palácio da Ajuda (1892-1833)*, Lisboa, Academia Nacional de Belas-Artes, 1936.

COUCHOT, Edmond – **Tecnologie dans l'art de la photographie a la realité virtuelle**. Paris: Éditions Jacqueline Chambon, 1998.

Idem – **L'Art numérique**. Paris: Flammarion, 2003.

Idem – **Des Images du temps et des machines dans les arts et la communication**. Paris: Éditions Jacquiline Chambon, 2007.

COVEY, Preston K. – Art or Forgery? The Strange Case of Han Van Meegeren. The Journal of Computing in Higher Education. Vol. 2, n° 1 (1990), p. 2-31.

COWARD, Harold – Taoism and Jung: Synchronicity and the Self. Philosophy East and West, Vol. 46, n.° 4 (1996), pp. 477-495.

CRUZ, António João – A matéria de que é feita a cor. Os pigmentos utilizados em pintura e a sua identificação e caracterização. 1.os Encontros de Conservação e Restauro – Tecnologias. Instituto Politécnico de Tomar, Tomar. Vol. 1 (2000), pp. 1-25.

CRUZ, José Gomes da, *Carta Apologetica y Analytica, que pela ingenuidade da pintura, em quanto sciencia escreveu...*, Lisboa, Na Regia Offic. Sylviana: Academia Real, 1752.

CUNHA, Rodrigo Sobral – **Sintra, Raul Lino**. Lisboa: Colares Editora, 2014.

D

D'ALLEVA, Anne, Methods & Theories of Art History, London, Laurence King Publishing, 2005.

DANTO, Arthur C. – The End of ARt: A Philosophical Defense. History and Theory. Vol. 37, No. 4 (1998), pp. 127-143.

DAICHENDT, James, *Artist Scholar: Reflections on Writing and Research*, Bristol, Intellect Ltd, 2011.

DAMISCH, Hubert, *A Theory of Cloud: toward a history of painting*, Stanford, Stanford University Press, 2002.

DANÉTIS, Daniel, *Pratiques artistiques et pratiques de recherche*, Paris, L'Harmattan, 2007.

DAVIES, Henry H., 'Origen's Theory of Knowledge', in The American Journal of Theology, Volume 2, Number 4, 1898, pp. 737-762.

DELBOURGO, S., 'Sauver l'Art? Conserver: Analyser: Restaurer by François Schweizer: Anne Rinuy', in Studies in Conservation, Volume 28, Number 2, 1983, pp. 95-96.

DERUYVER, Debra; EVANS, Jennifer – Digital Junction. <u>Amrican Quarterly</u>. Vol. 58, No. 3 (2006), pp. 943-980.

DESWARTE-ROSA, Sylvie; CHICÓ, Maria Alice – As Imagens das Idades do Mundo de Fransico de Holanda. Lisboa: Imprensa Nacional-Casa da Moeda, 1987.

DESWARTE, Sylvie – Ideias e imagens em Portugal na época dos descobrimentos: Francisco de Holanda e a teoria da arte. Lisboa: Difel, 1992.

DIAS, Fernando Rosa, 'Mário Eloy, que Expressionismo', in *Colóquio. Artes*, Número 107, 1995, pp. 36-42.

Idem, 'O expressionismo e a estética do feio', in *O feio para além do belo*, Lisboa, Centro de Filosofia da Universidade de Lisboa, 2012, pp. 147-155.

Idem, *Ecos expressionistas na pintura portuguesa entre-guerras (1914-1940)*, Lisboa, Campo da Comunicação, 2011.

DIDEROT, Denis, ALEMBERT, Jean Le Rond d'& MOUCHON, Pierre, *Encyclopédie*, Paris, Briasson, 1751.

Idem, Essais sur la peinture: salons de 1759, 1761, 1763, Paris, Hermann, 1984.

Idem, Salon de 1765, Paris, Hermann, 1984.

DIXON, Deborah P. – Creating the Semi-Living: On Politics, Aesthetics and the More-than-Human. <u>Transaction of the Institute of British Geographares</u>. Vol. 34, No. 4 (2009), pp. 411-425.

DORRELL, Peter – **Photography in archaeology and Conservation**. Cambridge: Cambridge University Press, 1989.

DOWNING, Cristine – Sigmund Freud and the Mythological Tradition. <u>Journal of the American Academy of Religion</u>. Vol. 43, n° 1 (1975), pp. 3-14.

DRESNER, Eli & HERRING, Susan C., 'Functions of the Non-Verbal in CMC: Emotions and Illocutionary Force, in Communication Theory, in press, University of Indiana, Available at http://info.ils.indiana.edu/~herring/emoticons.pdf [12-01-2015].

DÜRER, Albrecht, *The Painter's Manual*, Connecticut, Abaris Books, 1977.

DUVAL, M. & CUYER, E., *Histoire de l'anatomie, les maîtres, les livres et les écorchés*, Paris, M.H. May, 1899.

DUVE, Thierry de, *Kant after Duchamp*, Cambridge, M.I.T. Press, 1996.

DUVE, Thierry de, 'The Readymade and the Tube of Paint: Marcel Duchamp, Still Unraveling', in *Artforum*, Volume 24, Number 9, 1986, pp. 110-121.

E

ECO, Humberto, Como se faz uma tese em ciências humanas, Lisboa, Presença, 1988.

ELKINS, James, *Artists wirh PhDs (On the new Doctoral Degree in Studio Art)*, Washington DC, New Academia, 2009.

ELKINS, James, 'Piero della Francesca and the Renaissance Proof of Linear Perspective', in Art Bulletin, Volume 69, Number 2, 1987, pp. 220-230.

ESTÉVEZ, Alberto T. – The Genetic Creation of Bioluminescent Plants for Urban and Domestic Use. Leonardo. Vol. 40, No. 1 (2007), pp. 18-19.

ETHERINGTON, Kim, *Becoming a Reflexive Researcher: Using Our Selves in Research*, London, Jessica Kingsleu Pub., 2004.

EVANS, Elizabeth C., 'The Study of Physiognomy in the Second Century A.D.', in Transactions and Proceedings of the American Philolofical Association, Volume 72, 1941, pp. 96-108.

F

FARIA, Alberto, *A colecção de Desenho Antigo da Faculdade de Belas Artes de Lisboa (1830-1935): tradição, formação e gosto*, Dissertação de Mestrado em Museologia e Museografia, Faculdade de Belas-Artes da Universidade de Lisboa, 2008.

FARIA, Miguel, O ensino das Belas Artes em Portugal nas vésperas da fundação da Academia, Lisboa, Universidade Autónoma de Lisboa, 2000.

FARIES, Molly – Analytical capabilities of infrared reflectography: an art historian's perspective. In BERRIE, Barbara, RENÉ DE LA RIE, Etienne, TOMLINSON, Jannis; WINTER, John (Coord.) Scientific Examination of Art: Modern Techniques in Conservation and Analysis. Washington DC: National Academies Press, 2005, pp. 87–104.

FERRÃO, Hugo – Mitologia tecnológica: Cyberart – discurso Cyberpunk. Arte Teoria. Vol. 1, No. 1 (2000), pp. 60-69.

Idem – Ciberespaço e a arquitectura dos "não lugares" habitados por "homens sem qualidades". Arte Teoria. Vol. 1, No. 1 (2005), pp. 179-190.

Idem – Hipertexto, axis mundi das manifestações tecno-artísticas Arte Teoria. Vol. 1, No. 6 (2005), pp. 31-40.

Idem – Pintura como hipertexto do visível: instauração do tecno-imaginário do citor. Lisboa: Faculdade de Belas-Artes da Universidade de Lisboa, 2007. Tese de Doutoramento em Belas-Artes, especialidade de Pintura.

Idem – Imersão tecnológica e desertificação metafísica, ilhas e arquipélagos românticos. Arte Teoria. Vol. 1, No. 9 (2007), pp. 152-163.

Idem – Invisible network, novas fronteiras artísticas da interação com superfícies e objectos inteligentes. Circunvoluções digitais. Vol. 2, No. 1 (2010), pp. 49-59.

Idem – A cibercultura e os desafios das novas aprendizagens. 1ª Conferência Internacional em Design e Artes Gráficas. Lisboa, 2011, pp. 60-66.

FIGUEIREDO, José de, Arte portuguesa primitiva, Lisboa, [s.n.], 1910.

FILIPE, Patrícia Trindade – <u>Alternatica um: Respostas Polémicas à Alternativa Zero</u>. Lisboa: Faculdade de Belas-Artes da Universidade de Lisboa, 2008. Dissertação de Mestrado em Estudos Curatoriais.

FINOCCHIARO, Maurice A., 'Galileo and the Philosophy of Science', in PSA: Proceedings of the Biennal Meeting of the Philosophy of Science Association, Volume 1, 1976, pp. 130-139.

FOUCAULT, Michael – **Introduction to Kant's Anthropology**. New York: Semiotext, 2008.

FRANÇA, José-Augusto – **A Arte em Portugal no século XX: 1911-1961**. Lisboa: Livros Horizonte, 2009.

Idem, A arte em Portugal no século XIX, Lisboa, Bertrand, 1981.

Idem, *Os modernistas na Academia*, Lisboa, Academia Nacional de Belas Artes, 1984.

FRANÇA, Alfredo & VALENÇA, Francisco, Paneleida, Lisboa, A Peninsular, 1926.

FREEMAN, John, *Blood Sweat and Theory: Research Through Practice in Performance (Music + Performing Arts)*, Oxford, Libri Publishing, 2010.

FREUD, Sigmund – **Essais de psychanalyse**. Paris: Payot, 1979.

Idem, A interpretação dos sonhos, Lisboa, Relógio de Água, 2009.

G

GALDSTON, Iago – A Critical Summary and Review. <u>Isis</u>. Vol. 40, n° 4 (1949), pp. 316-327.

GALILEI, Galileu, Sidereus Nuncius: O mensageiro das estrelas, Lisboa, Fundação Calouste Gulbenkian, 2010.

GARRETT, Almeida, O retrato de Vénus e Estudos da História Letteraria, Porto, Viúva Moré, 1867.

GHANI, Dahnlan Bin Abdul – The Study of Semiotics Wayang Kulit Theatre in Malay Culture Society. Estudios sobre el Mensaje Presiodístico. Vol. 18, n.° 1 (2012), pp. 321-335.

GHOSH, Sampa; BANERJEE, Utpal K. – Indian puppets. New Delhi: Abhinav Publications, 2012, p. 15.

GIGLIOTTI, Carol, 'Bridge to, Bridge from: The Arts, Technology and Education', in Leonardo, Volume 31, Number 2, 1998, pp. 89-92.

GILLIES, Jean, 'Timeless Space of Edward Hopper', in Art Journal, Volume 31, Number 4, 1972, pp. 407.

GINO, Francesca; PIERCE, Lamar – Lying to Level the Playing Field: Why People May Dishonestly Help or Hurt Others to Create Equity. Journal of Business Ethics. Vol. 95, Supplement 1 (2010), pp. 89-103.

GINO, Francesca; WILTERMUTH, Scott S. – **Evil Genius? How Dishonesty Can Lead to Greater Creativity**. Available athttp://www.pscience.com/wp-content/uploads/2014/02/EvilGenius.pdf [17-05-2015].

GODINHO, Aulo-Gélio Severino – **Raul Lino: o artista e a obra**. Porto: Associação Portuense de Ex-Libris, 1972.

GÓMEZ, Maria Luisa – **La restauración: Examen científico aplicado a la conservación de obras de arte**. Madrid: Catedra-Cuadernos Arte, 2008.

GOMES, Manuel Teixeira – Cartas a Columbano. Lisboa: Portugália, 1957.

GOMES, Paulo Varela, A Confissão de Cyrillo: Estudos de História da Arte e da Aquitectura, Lisboa, Hiena, 1992.

GÓMEZ, Maria Luisa, La restauración: Examen científico aplicado a la conservación de obras de arte, Madrid, Catedra-Cuadernos Arte, 2008.

GONÇALVES, António Nogueira, O mestre dos túmulos dos reis, Coimbra, Faculdade de Letras da Universidade, 1975.

GONÇALVES, Flávio, História da arte: iconografia e crítica, Lisboa, Imprensa Nacional Casa da Moeda, 1990.

GONSE, L., 'Manet', in Gazette des Beaux-Arts, Paris, École des Beaux Arts, juillet, 1884.

GRAY, Carole & MALINS, Julian, Visualizing Research: A Guide To The Research Process In Art And Design, London, Ashgate Pub Ltd, 2004.

GRAY, Carole & MALINS, Julian, Visualizing Research: A Guide to the Research Process in Art and Design, Oxford, Ashgate, 2004.

GROSSMAN, Kathryn M. – Playing Surrealist Games: Parataxis and Creativity. The French Review. Vol. 52, No. 5 (1979), pp. 700-707.

GROSSMAN, Ruth B. & TAGER-FLUSBERG, Helen, 'Reading faces for information about words and emotions in adolescents with autism', in Research in Autism Spectrum Disorders, Volume 2, 2008, pp. 681-695.

GUERLAC, Suzanne – Bataille in Theory: Afterimages (Lascaux). Diacritics. Vol. 26, n° 2 (1996), pp. 6-17.

GUILLAIN, R., 'Japanese Uncertainties', in International Affairs, Volume 26, Number 3, 1950, pp. 329-338.

GUSMÃO, Adriano de, O Nuno Gonçalves da Phaidon: Erros, omissões e plágios, Lisboa, Europa-América, [s.d.].

GUSMÃO, Artur Nobre de, Românico português do noroeste: alguns motivos geométricos na escultura decorativa, Lisboa, Vega, 1992.

GUYER, Paul, 'Free Play and True Well-Being: Herder's Critique of Kant's Aesthetics', in The Journal of Aesthetics and Art Criticism, Volume 65, Number 4, 2007, pp. 353-368.

H

HAIN, Miraslov, BARTI, Jan; JACKO, Viado – Multispectral analysis of cultural heritage artefacts. Measurement Science Review. Vol. 3, n° 1 (2003), pp. 9–12.

HAKER, Helene, KAWOHL, Wolfram, HERWIG, Uwe & ROSSIER, Wulf, 'Mirror neuron activity during contagious yawning-an fMRI study', in Brain Imaging and Behaviour, Volume 7, Issue 1, pp. 28-34.

HANSEN, Miriam Bratu, 'Benjamin's Aura', in Critical Inquiry, Volume 34, Number 2, 2008, pp. 336-375.

HARCOURT, Glenn – Andreas Vesalius and the Anatomy of Antique Sculpture. Representations, Vol. 1, n° 1 (1987), pp. 28-61

HARRIS, John P. – Plato's "Ion" and the End of his "Symposium". Illinois Classical Studies. Vol. 26, n° 1 (2011), pp. 81-100.

HEGEL, G.W.F. – The Philosophy of Plato. The Journal of Speculative Philosophy. Vol. 4, n° 3 (1870), pp. 225-268.

HEGEL, Friedrich, Estética, Lisboa, Guimarães Editores, 1993.

HEIDEGGER, Martin – **Ser e tempo**. Petrólopis: Vozes, 1998.

HEIDEL, William Arthur, 'ΠερὶΦύσεως. A Study of the Conception of Nature among the Pre-Socratics', in Proceedings of the American Academy of Arts and Sciences, Volume 45, Number 4, 1910, pp. 79-133.

HERCULANO, Alexandre, Opúsculos: Monumentos Pátrios, Volume 2, Lisboa, Viúva Bertrand, 1908.

HERTZ, Paul – Art, Code, and the Engine of Change. Art Journal. Vol. 68, No. 1 (2009), pp. 58-75.

HILMER, Brigitte – Being Hegelian after Danto. History and Theory. Vol. 37, No. 4 (1998), pp. 71-86.

HINCHMAN, Lewis P. – The Origins of Human Rights: A Hegelian Perspective. The Western Political Quarterly. Vol. 37, n° 1 (1984), pp. 7-31.

HINCHMAN, Lewis P., 'The Origins of Human Rights: A Hegelian Perspective', in The Western Political Quarterly, Volume 37, Number 1, 1984, pp. 7-31.

HOLANDA, Francisco de, *Do tirar pelo natural*, Lisboa, Livros Horizonte, 1984.

Idem, *Da Ciência do Desenho*, Lisboa, Livros Horizonte, Capítulo 1.°, *fl. 34r* e *fl. 34v.°*.

Idem, *Da Pintura Antiga*, Lisboa, Imprensa Nacional, [s.d.] (original de 1548).

Idem – Diálogos em Roma. Lisboa: Livros Horizonte, 1984.

Idem – Da Pintura Antiga. Lisboa: Imprensa Nacional-Casa da Moeda, 1986.

Idem – A ideia na Pintura. Eldorado, Lisboa, 1980, pp. 56/57.

HOWE, Susan – The End of Art. Archives of American Art Journal. Vol. 14, No. 4 (1974), pp. 2-7.

HUNT, Peter, *Revolution in painting*, North Carolina Museum of Art. Available athttp://ncartmuseum.org/pdf/revolution-supplement.pdf [26-09-2014].

I

IWASAKI, Noriko, 'Learning L2 Japanese "Politeness" and "Impoliteness": Young American Men's Dilemmas during Study Abroad', in Japanese Language and Literature, Volume 45, Number 1, 2011, pp. 67-106.

IZZO, Francesca Caterina, *20th artists' oil paints: a chemical-physical survey: a chemical-physical survey*, Tese de doutoramento em Ciência Química, Università Ca' Foscari Venezia, 2011.

J

JANTZEN, Éric, Traité Pratique de Perspective de photographie et de dessin appliqués à l'architecture et au paysagei, Paris, La Villette Eds De, 1996.

JONES, Gwyneth – Art, Forward Slash, Science. PMLA. Vol. 119, No. 3 (2004), pp. 526-529.

JONES, Peter, 'Museums and the Meanings of Their Contents', in New Literary History, Volume 23, Number 4, 1992, pp. 911-921.

JOSEPHNS, Lawrence – The Freudian Superego. Journal of Religion and Health. Vol. 33, n° 2 (1994), pp. 149-151.

JUNG, Carl – The red book. New York: W. W. Norton & Company, 2009.

Idem – Tipos psicológicos. Rio de Janeiro: Zahar, 1974.

JÚNIOR, José Amaro, *Mestre Veloso Salgado Pintor: Mestre de* pintores, Lisboa, Elóquios, 1948.

K

KANT, Immanuel – **Crítica da Razão Pura**. Lisboa: Fundação Calouste Gulbenkian, 1994.

Idem – **Crítica da Faculdade do Juízo**. Lisboa: Imprensa Nacional Casa da Moeda, 1992.

KAPLAN, Robert – Madness and James Joyce. <u>Australasian Psychiatry</u>. Vol. 10, n° 2 (2002), pp. 172-176.

KARASMANIS, Vassilis – Plato's Republic: The Line and the Cave. <u>Apeiron: a Journal of Ancient Philosophy and Science</u>. Vol. 21, n° 3 (1988), pp. 147-171.

KAZADOY, Ruth L. – The Origin of Early Christian Book Illumination: The State of the Question. Gesta. Vol. 10, n,° 2 (1971), pp. 33-40.
KENDON, Adam, 'Gesture', in Annual Review of Anthropology, Volume 26, 1997, pp. 109-128.
KENNINGTON, Richard – The Finitude of Descartes' Evil Genius. <u>Journal of the History of Ideas</u>. Vol. 32, n° 3 (1971), pp. 441-446.

KERINSKA, Nikoleta – <u>Art et intelligence artificielle: dans le contexte d'une expérimentations artistique</u>. Paris: Univeristé Sorbonne, Panthéon, 2014. Tese de doutoramento em Ciências da Arte.

KERSHAW, Baz & NICHOLSON, Helen, *Research Methods in Theatre and Performance (Research Methods for the Arts and Humanities)*, Edinburgh, Edinburgh University Press, 2010.

KINGS, Steven – Jung's Hermeneutics of Scripture. <u>The Journal of Religion</u>. Vol. 77, n° 2 (1997), pp. 233-251.

KIRSHENBLATT-GIMBLETT, Barbara, Destination Culture. Tourism, Museums and Heritage. Berkeley, University of California Press, 1998.
KLEIN, Norman M. – Building Blade Runner. <u>Social Text</u>. Vol. 1, No. 28 (1991), pp. 147-152.

KNOWLES, Gary & COLE, Ardra, *Handbook of the Arts in Qualitative Research: Perspectives, Methodologies, Examples and Issues*, London, Sage Pub., 2007.

KRAUSS, Rosalind E. – **The Originality of the Avant-Garde and other modernist myths**. 9ª Ed. Cambridge: The MIT Press, 1994.

KUBLER, George – **A arquitectura portuguesa chã: entre as especiarias e os diamantes, 1521-1706.** Lisboa: Vega, 1988.

KUBLER, George Alexander, A forma do tempo: observações sobre a história dos objectos, Lisboa, Vega, 1991.

L

LACAN, Jacques – **O seminário.** Rio de Janeiro: Jorge Zahar Editor, 1995.

LACERDA, Aarão de, História da arte em Portugal, Porto, Portucalense, 1953.

LANGER, Carl – **Anatomie der äussen formen des menschlichen korpers.** Wien: Toeplitx & Deuticke, 1884.

LEANDRO, Sandra – Teoria e Crítica de Arte em Portugal no final do século XIX. Seminários de Estudos de Arte: Estados da Forma I. Évora: Edições Eu é que sei, 2007, p. 39.

LEBEN, Ulrich, *Object Design in the Age of Enlightnment,* Los Angeles, The J. Paul Getty Museum, 2005.

Idem, *L'École Royale Gratuite de Dessin de Paris,* Saint-Rémy-en-l'Eau, Éditions Monelle Hayot, 2004.

LEBEN, Ulrich & GILLESPIE, Susan, 'New Light on the École Royale Gratuite de Dessin: The Years 1766-1815', in *Studies in the Decorative Arts,* Volume 1, Number 1, 1993, pp. 99-118.

LEMERT, Charles C. – Language, Structure, and Measurement: Structuralist Semiotics and Sociology. American Journal of Sociology. Vol. 84, n.º 4 (1979), pp. 929-957.

LEWIS, Geoffry, 'The Role of Museums and the Professional Code of Ethics', in Runninf a Museum: A Practical Handbook, Paris, ICOM, pp. 1-16.

LIFSHITZ, M., The Philosophy of Art of Karl Marx, New York, Critics Group, 1938.

LINO, Raul – Projeto de reconstrução dos Paços do Concelho, Setúbal, 1928, 19 desenhos de arquitetura, 1 desenho técnico de engenharia e memórias descritivas, Arquivo da Fundação da Biblioteca Calouste Gulbenkian.

Idem – **Casas Portuguesas: alguns apontamentos sobre o arquitectar das casas simples**. Lisboa: Cotovia, 1992.

Idem – **A nossa casa: apontamentos sobre o bom gosto na construção das casas**. Lisboa: Ottosgrafica, 1923.

Idem – **Projecto de ampliação do Museu de Arte Contemporânea, Rua Serpa Pinto, Lisboa, 1930**. Série de 7 desenhos de arquitectura, Arquivo da Biblioteca da Fundação Calouste Gulbenkian. [11-05-2015].

Idem – **Exposição Colonial Internacional de Paris**. Série de 15 desenhos de arquitectura, 4 fotografias, programa, memórias descritivas, caderno de encargos, decoração interior dos pavilhões e artigos de imprensa, Arquivo da Fundação da Biblioteca Calouste Gulbenkian. [11-05-2015].

LIPOVETSKY, Gilles; SERROY, Jean – **A Cultura-Mundo. Resposta a uma sociedade desorientada**. Tradução de Victor Silva. Lisboa: Edições 70, 2010.

LISBOA, Maria Helena, *As academias e escolas de Belas Artes e o ensino artístico (1836-1910)*, Lisboa, Colibri, 2007.

LOTZE, Hermann, Outlines of Aesthetics, trans. e ed. por G. Ladd, Boston, 1885, p. 20.

LOUSÃ, Teresa, *Francisco de Holanda e a Ascensão do Pintor*, Tese de doutoramento, FBAUL, 2001.

Idem – O pintor como Deus in Terris: de Ficino a Francisco de Holanda. Arte Teoria, Lisboa, 2000, N.° 14/15, pp. 23-30.

Idem – A defesa do estatuto do artista na obra de Francisco de Holanda. Arte Teoria, Lisboa, 2000, N.º 6, pp. 94-105.

LOMBARDINI, A. – **Manual de Anatomia Plastica**. Lisboa: Tavares Cardoso & Irmão, 1903.

LORENA, Mercês, ANTUNES, Vanessa; OLIVEIRA, Maria José – O desenho dentro da pintura do tríptico de Coimbra. Cadernos de Conservação e Restauro – O Tríptico de Santa Clara. Vol. 1, n° 8 (2010), p. 68.

LYOTARD, Jean-François – **L'inhumain**. Paris: Galilée, 1988.

LYALL, A.C. – Brahmanisn. The North American Review. Vol. 171, n.º 529 (1900), pp. 920-934.

LYONS, Lucy, 'Walls Are Not My Friends: Issues Surrounding the Dissemination of Practice-led Research within Appropriate and Relevant Contexts', in Working Papers in Art and Design, Number 4, 2006.

M

MACEDO, Diogo de, A escultura portuguesa nos séculos XVII e XVIII, Lisboa, Ocidente, 1945.

MACHADO, Cyrillo Volkmar, Collecção de memórias relativas ás vidas dos pintores, e escultores, architectos e gravadores portuguezes, e dos estrangeiros que estiverão em Portugal, Lisboa, Imprensa de Victorino Rodrigues da Silva, 1823.

MACKINNON, Edward – The Development of Kant's Conception of Scientific Explanation. <u>Proceedings of the Biennal Meeting of the Philosophy of Science Association</u>. Vol. 1 (1978), pp. 18-30.

MCGINN, Bernard, 'The Changing Shape of Late Medieval Mysticism', in Church History, Volume 65, Number 2, 1996, pp. 197-219.

MACKINNON, Edward, 'The Development of Kant's Conception of Scientific Explanation', in Proceedings of the Biennal Meeting of the Philosophy of Science Association, Volume 1, 1978, pp. 18-30.

MACLEOD, Katy, *Thinking Through Art: Reflections on Art as Research (Innovations in Art and Design)*, London, Routledge, 2009.

MACLEOD, Katy & HOLDRIDGE, Lin, 'Writing and the PhD in fine art', in *The Routledge companion to research in the arts*, New York, Routledge, 2010, pp. 353-367.

MADOFF, Steven Henry, *Art school (propositions for the 21st century)*, London, M.I.T. Press, 2009.

MAIO, Fernanda, '"Vidas reais, gente real": A re-presentação de outros na arte no espaço público', in Revista Crítica de Ciências Sociais, Número 75, 2006, pp. 95-115.

MAIRINGER, Franz – The ultraviolet and fluorescence study of paintings and manuscripts. In CREAGH, Dudley & BRADLEY,

David (Ed.) <u>Radiation in Art and Archaeometry</u>. Amsterdam: Elsevier, 2000, pp. 40-55.

Idem – UV-, IR- and X-ray imaging. In JANSSENS Koen; VAN GRIEKEN, Rene (Ed.) <u>Non-Destructive Micro-analysis of Cultural Heritage Materials</u>. Amsterdam: Elsevier, 2004, pp. 15-71.

MARKL, Dagoberto, O essencial sobre Nuno Gonçalves, Lisboa, Imprensa Nacional Casa da Moeda, 1987.

MARKOWICZ, Andrzej – Interaction of photons with matter. In DEKKER, Marcel (Ed.) <u>Handbook of X-Ray Spectrometry</u>. New York: Marcel Dekker Inc, 1993, pp. 17-21.

MASSING, Ann, 'From Books of Secrets to Encyclopedias: Painting Techniques in France between 1600 and 1800', In WALLERT, Arie, HERMENS, Erma & PEEK, Marja (Ed.) *Historical Painting Techniques, Materials, and Studio Practice*, The Getty Conservation Institute, Kansas, 1995, pp. 20-29.

MATIAS, Vanessa Otero, *Historically Accurate reconstructions and characterisation of chrome yellow pigments*, Dissertação de Mestrado em Ciências da Conservação, Faculdade de Ciências e Tecnologia da Universidade Nova de Lisboa, Monte de Caparica, 2010.

MATTEINI, Mauro; MOLES, Arcangelo – **Scienza e restauro**. Firenze: Nardini Editore, 1984.

Idem – **La química en la restauración – Los Materiales del arte Pictórico**. San Sebastián: Editorial Nerea, 2001.

MCCLELLAN, Andrew L., 'The Musée du Louvre as Revolutionary Metaphor During the Terror', in The Art Bulletin, Volume 1, Number 2, 1988, pp. 300-313.

MCGANN, Jerome – Culture and Technology: The Way We Live Now, What Is to Be Done?. <u>New Literary History</u>. Vol. 36, No. 1 (2005), pp. 71-82.

MCKNIGHT, Jeanne – Unlocking the World-Hoard: Madness, Identity and Creativity in James Joyce. <u>James Joyce Quarterly</u>. Vol. 14, n° 4 (1977), pp. 420-435.

MCNAMARA, Kevin R. – "Blade Runner's" Post-Individual Worldspace. Contemporary Literature. Vol. 38, No. 3 (1997), pp. 422-446.

MEANS, Loren – Autonomous Robots That Paint. YLEM Journal – Artists Using Science and Technology. Vol. 27, No. 6 (2007), pp. 2-14.

MENN, Stephen – Aristotle and Plato on God as Nous and as the Good. The Review of Metaphysics. Vol. 45, n° 3 (1992), pp. 543-573.

MERLEAU-PONTY, Maurice, Fenomenologia da percepção, São Paulo, Martins Fontes, 1994.

MERRITT, Richard K. – From Memory Arts to the New Code Paradigm: The Artist as Engineer of Virtual Information Space and Virtual Experience. Leonardo. Vol. 34, No. 5 (2001), pp. 403-408.

MESQUITA, Marilisa – O sorriso humano. Lisboa: Faculdade de Belas-Artes de Lisboa, 2012. Dissertação de Mestrado em Anatomia Artística.

MESQUITA, Marilisa, O sorriso humano, Tese de Mestrado em Anatomia Artística, Faculdade de Belas-Artes da Universidade de Lisboa, Lisboa, 2011.

MICHEL, Régis & WRIGLEY, Richard, 'Diderot and Modernity', in Oxford Art Journal, Volume 8, Number 2, 1985, pp. 36-51.

MILLS, Allan A., 'Vermeer and the Camera Obscura: Some Practical Considerations', in Leonardo, Volume 31, Number 3, 1998, pp. 213-218.

MOLNAR, F., 'Experimental Aesthetics or the Science of Art', in Leonardo, Volume 7, Number 1, 1974, pp. 23-26.

MONICO, Letizia et al., 'Degradation Process of Lead Chromate in Paintings by Vincent van Gogh Studied by Means of Synchrotron X-Ray Spectromicroscopy and Related Materials. 2. Original Paint Layer Samples', in Analytical Chemistry, Volume 83, Number 4, pp. 1224-1231.

Idem, 'Degradation Process of Lead Chromate in Paintings by Vincent van Gogh Studied by Means of Synchrotron X-Ray Spectromicroscopy and Related Materials. 3. Synthesis, Characterization and Detection of Different Crystal Forms of the Chrome Yellow Pigment', in Analytical Chemistry, Volume 85, Number 2, pp. 851-859.

MONTEZ, Paulino, 'Do ensino de Belas Artes em Portugal através dos séculos', in Boletim da Escola Superior de Belas Artes de Lisboa, Número 2, 1960, pp. 9-26.

MOOG, Viana – Eça de Queiroz e o século XIX. Porto Alegre: Livraria do Globo, 1939, p. 153.

MOREAUX, Arnould – **Anatomia artistica del hombre : compendio de anatomia osea y muscular.** Madrid: Ediciones Norma, 1988.

MOREIRA, Rafael, A arquitectura militar do Renascimento em Portugal, Coimbra, Epatur, 1981.

MOURÃO, José Augusto, FRANCO, José Eduardo & SERRÃO, Vítor (Coord.), *Monjas Dominicanas. Presença, Arte e Património em Lisboa*, Lisboa, Alétheia Editores, 2008.

MOURELATOS, Alexander P., 'Pre-Socratic Origins of the Principle that There are No Origins from Nothing', in The Journal of Philosophy, Volume 78, Number 11, 1981, pp. 649-665.

MOUSTAKAS, Clark E., *Heuristic research: design, methodology and applications*, Newbury Park, Sage Pub., 1990.

MUNRO, Thomas, 'Knowledge and Control in the Field of Aesthetics', in The Journal of Aesthetics and Art Criticism, Volume 1, Number 1, 1941, p. 1-12.

N

NASCIMENTO, Susana Lemos de, *A importância do corpo humano no ensino do Desenho na Escola de Belas-Artes de Lisboa no século XX: antes e depois da integração na Universidade de Lisboa,* Dissertação de Mestrado em Desenho, Faculdade de Belas-Artes da Universidade de Lisboa, 2006.

NELSON, Thedor – **Computer Lib / Dream Machines**. New York: Microsoft edition, 1987.

NETO, Maria João – **James Murphy e o restauro do Mosteiro de Santa Maria da Vitória no Século XIX**. Lisboa: Editorial Estampa, 1996.

Idem – Raul Lino ao serviço da Direcção-Geral dos Edifícios e Monumentos Nacionais. Artis. Vol. 1, n° 1 (2002), pp. 253-269.

NESBIT, Molly – Ready-Made Originals: The Duchamp Model. <u>October</u>. Vol. 37, No. 1 (1986), pp. 53-64.

NICHOLS, Mary P. – Philosophy and Empire: On Socrates and Alcibiades in Plato's "Symposium". <u>Polity</u>. Vol. 39, n° 4 (2007), pp. 502-521.

Idem – Socrates' Contest with the Poets in Plato's Symposium. <u>Political Theory</u>. Vol. 32, n° 2 (2004), pp. 184-206.

NIETZSCHE, Friedrich – **Humano, demasiado humano: um livro para espíritos livres**. Lisboa: Relógio D'Água, 1997.

Idem, *A origem da tragédia*, Lisboa, Guimarães Editores, 1994.

NOGUEIRA, Isabel – Alternativa Zero (1977): o reafirmar da possibilidade da criação. <u>Caderno do CEIS20</u>. Vol. 1, No. 7 (2008), pp. 9-28.

NORDEN, Martin F. – The Avant-Garde Cinema of the 1920s: Connections to Futurism, Precisionism, and Suprematism. <u>Leonardo</u>. Vol. 17, No. 2 (1884), pp. 108-112.

NUNES, Filipe, *A Arte da pintura, symmetria, e perspectiva*, Porto, Paisagem, 1982.

O
OLEIRO, João Manuel Bairrão, Novos elementos para a história de "aeminium", Coimbra, Coimbra Editora, 1952.
ORS, Eugénio de, Du Baroque, Paris, Gallimard, 1935.
ORTI, Maria Angustias – **Los métodos de análisis físico-químicos y la historia del arte**. Granada: Universidad de Granada, 1994.

ORTIGÃO, Maria João – Aurélia de Sousa em contexto: A cultura artística no fim de século, Volume I, 2006, p. 111. Dissertação de Doutoramento em Ciências da Arte, Faculdade de Belas-Artes da Universidade de Lisboa.
Idem – Eça de Queirós e Ramalho Ortigão: entre a Geração de Setenta e os Vencidos da Vida. Chiado, Atas de Conferências. Lisboa:

Faculdade de Belas-Artes da Universidade de Lisboa – CIEBA (2010), pp. 56-61

ORTIGÃO, Ramalho – **O culto da arte em Portugal**. Lisboa: A.M. Pereira, 1896.

Idem – Últimas Farpas. Rio de Janeiro: Francisco Alves, 1916.

Idem – O Mistério da Estrada de Sintra. Lisboa: Livros do Brasil, 1970.

Idem – Farpas completas. Mem Martins: Círculo de Leitores, 2006.

OZMENT, Steven E., '"Homo Viator": Luther and Late Medieval Theology', in The Harvard Theological Review, Volume 62, Number 3, 1969, pp. 275-287.

P

PAMPLONA, Mª Ángeles, *Investigarte. Andamios para una construcción de la invesstigación en Bellas Artes,* Madrid, Universidade Complutense de Madrid, 2003.

PANOFSKY, Erwin, Significado nas artes visuais, São Paulo, Perspectiva, 1979.

Idem, 'On the Relationship of Art History and Art Theory: Towards the Possibility of a Fundamental System of Concepts for a Science of Art', in Critical Inquiry, Volume 35, Number 1, 2008, pp. 43-71.

PARLETT, Malcolm & HAMILTON, David, 'Evaluation as Illumination: A New Approach to the Study of Innovative Programmes', in Evaluation Studies Review Anual, Volume 1, 1976, pp. 140-157.

PARTEE, Morriss Henry – Inspiration in the Aesthetics of Plato. The Journal of Aesthetics and Art Criticism. Vol. 30, n°1 (1971), pp. 87-95.

PARTNER, Nancy F. – No Sex, No Gender. Speculum. Vol. 68, n° 2 (1993), pp. 419-443.

PASSOS, Carlos de – Esboço dum vocabulário aryano: Vedas, Mahabarata e Ramayana. Coimbra: Imprensa da Universidade, 1917, pp. 20-23

PEASE, Murray – A Note on the Radiography of Paintings. The Metropolitan Museum of Art Bulletin. New Series. Vol. 4, n° 5 (1946), pp. 136-139.

PEDROSO, Joana, *Estudo da degradação de óleos secativos, em tintas de Amadeo de Souza-Cardoso, Silva Porto e Gustave Courbet,* Dissertação de mestrado em Conservação e Restauro, Universidade Nova de Lisboa, 2009.

PEIRCE, Charles Sanders, Semiótica, São Paulo, Pespectiva, 1977.

PENEDA, João Manuel – **O que é o belo?: comentário ao diálogo Hípias Maior**. Trabalho de síntese. Lisboa: Faculdade de Belas-Artes da Universidade de Lisboa, 1997.

Idem – Os paradoxos do sintoma e da sublimação: o contributo da teoria psicanalítica de Freud e de Lacan para a estética. Lisboa: Faculdade de Belas-Artes da Universidade de Lisboa, 2005. Tese de doutoramento em Belas Artes.

Idem, A formulação kantiana da problematicidade estética, Provas de aptidão pedagógica e capacidade científica, Faculdade de Belas-Artes da Universidade de Lisboa, 1997.

PEREIRA, Fernando António Baptista; DIAS, Fernando Rosa – Ciências da Arte e a Criação Artística: solidariedades para uma investigação em arte. Investigação em arte e design, Lisboa (2011), pp. 214-228.

PEREIRA, José Fernandes, A Cultura Artística Portuguesa, Sistema Clássico, Lisboa, [s.n.], 1999.

PEREIRA, Paulo, História da Arte Portuguesa, 3 Volumes, Lisboa, Círculo de Leitores, 1995.

PEVSNER, Nikolaus, Le academie d'art, Torino, Giulio Einaudi Editore, 1982.

PLATÃO – **Hípias Maior**. Coimbra: Instituto Nacional de Investigação Científica, 1985.

Idem – **O Banquete**. Lisboa: Edições 70, 1991.

Idem – **Íon**. Lisboa: Inquérito, 2000.

Idem – Fédon: Diálogo sobre a imortalidade da alma. Coimbra: Atlântida, 1947.

Idem – A República. Lisboa: Fundação Calouste Gulbenkian, 1983.

POLKA, Brayton – 'Freud, Science, and the Psychoanalytical Critique of Religion: The Paradox of Self-Referentiality', in *Journal of the American Academy of Religion*, Vol. 62, No. 1, 1994, pp. 59-83.

POLLOCK, John L. – What Am I? Virtual Machines and the Mind/Body Problem. Philosophy and Phenomenological Research. Vol. 76, No. 2 (2008), pp. 237-309.

POPPER, Karl, 'Knowledge without Authority (1960)', in Theory of Knowledge: Selectrions, MILLER, D. (Ed.), Princeton, Princeton University Press, 1985, pp. 46-57.

Idem 'Conhecimento Objectivo e Subjectivo', in O Conhecimento e o Problema Corpo-Mente, Lisboa, Edições 70, 1996, pp. 13- 43.

Idem, Conjectures and Refutation; The Growth of Scientific Knowledge, London, Routledge Classics, 2002.

Q

QUEIRÓS, Eça de – O mistério da estrada de Sintra. Lisboa: Livros do Brasil, 197?.

QUEIRÓS, Eça de; ORTIGÃO, Ramalho – As Farpas: Chronica Mensal da Política, das Letras e dos Costumes. Lisboa: Emprenza Litteraria Luso-Brazileira, 1883.

QUINET, Edgar, Mes vacances en Espagne, Paris, Libr. Germer-Bailliére, 1857.

QUIRINO, Ana Carolina – Sombra – do Vestígio ao Enigma. Lisboa: Faculdade de Belas-Artes da Universidade de Lisboa, 2011, p. 7. Tese de Mestrado em Pintura.

R

RACZNSKI, Le Comte A., Les Arts en Portugal, Paris, Jules Renouard et Cie. Libraires-Éditeurs, 1846.

Idem, Dictionnaire Historico-Artistique du Portugal, Paris, Jules Renouard et Cie. Libraires-Éditeurs, 1847.

RAILTON, Peter, 'The Affective Dog and Its Rational Tale: Intuition and Attunement', in Ethics, Volume 124, Number 4, 2014, pp. 813-859.

RAMOS, Artur, Retrato: o desenho da Presença, Lisboa, Campo da Comunicação, 2010.

RAMPLEY, Matthew, 'From Symbol to Allegory: Aby Warburg's Theory of Art', in The Art Bulletin, Volume 79, Number 1, 1997, pp. 41-55.

REIS, Vitor dos, O Rapto do Observador: Invenção, Representação e Percepção do Espaço Celestial na Pintura de Tectos em Portugal no Século XVIII, Tese de doutoramento em Belas Artes, especialidade em Cultura e Forma Visual, Faculdade de Belas-Artes da Universidade de Lisboa, Lisboa, 2006.

RÉNE DE LA RIE, Etienne – Fluorescence of paint and varnish layers (Part I). Studies in Conservation. Vol. 27, n° 1 (1982), pp. 1-7.

RIBEIRO, Irene – **Raul Lino: Pensador Nacionalista da arquitectura**. Lisboa: Faculdade de Arquitectura da Universidade do Porto publicações, 1994.

RIBEIRO, Rogério, *A aula de desenho: Academias dos Séc. XIX e XX das Escolas de Belas Artes*, Almada, Câmara Municipal, 1989.

RIBEIRO, Rúben, 'A Barra da Cidade do Porto. Breves Apontamentos', in *Atas do IX Encontro Nacional de Estudantes de História,* Porto, Faculdade de Letras da Universidade do Porto, Biblioteca digital, 2014, pp. 149-165. Available athttp://ler.letras.up.pt/uploads/ficheiros/12130.pdf [02-01-2015].

RICHER, Paul – **Canon des proportions du corps humain**. Paris: Libraire Ch. Delagrave, 1893.

RIPA, Cesare, *Iconologia: overo descrittione di diverse imagini cavate dall'antichità*, Hildesheim, Georg Olms, 2003.

ROBERTS, John, *The Intangibilities of Form: Skill and Deskilling in Art after the Readymade*, London, Verso, 2007.

RODRIGUES, Maria Dalila Aguiar – Modos de expressão na pintura portuguesa: O processo criativo de Vasco Fernandes (1500-1542). Coimbra: Faculdade de Letras da Universidade de Coimbra, 2000. Dissertação de Doutoramento.

ROUVIÉRE, H., Anatomie Humaine: Descriptive, topographique et fonctionnelle, Volume 1, 1948.

ROYCE, Josiah, 'Race Questions and Prejudice', in International Journal of Ethics, Volume 16, Number 3, 1906, pp. 265-288.

S

SACRAMENTO, Nuno, 'Artocracy: art, informal space, and social consequente ou simplesmente "far from reality"', in Arte & Sociedade, Lisboa, 2011, pp. 416-429.

SANTOS, Luís Reis, 'Paineis dos Mestres de Ferreirim de igrejas e conventros de Évora', in *Sep. de A cidade de Évora do Boletim da Câmara Municipal de Évora*, numerous 21 e 22, 1950, pp. 9-28.

SANTOS, Reinaldo dos, *Os primitivos portugueses: 1450-1550*, Lisboa, Academia Nacional de Belas Artes, 1940.

SANTOS, Pedro, O Trompe L'Oeil Barroco na Igreja do Menino Deus em Lisboa: métodos e técnicas, Tese de Doutoramento em Belas Artes, especialidade em Geometria, Faculdade de Belas-Artes da Universidade de Lisboa, Lisboa, 2014.

SANTOS, Reinaldo dos, L'art portugais, Lisbonne, Académie National des Beaux Arts, 1949.

SAUSSURE, Ferdinand de, Curso de linguística geral, Lisboa, Dom Quixote, 1992.

SAXE, Geoffrey B. – Piaget and Anthropology. American Anthropologist. Vol. 85, n° 1 (1983), pp. 136-143.

SCHATZBERG, Eric – From Art to Applied Science. Isis. Vol. 103, n° 3 (2012), pp. 555-563.

SCHLEIFER, Michael – Moral Education and Indoctrination. Ethics. Vol. 86, n° 2 (1976), pp. 154-163.

SCHNERR, Walter J. – Ramalho Ortigão and the Generation of 1870. Hispania. Vol. 44, n.° 1, (1961), pp. 42-46.

SCHOPENHAUER, Arthur, *El mundo como voluntad y representación*, Mexico, Porrúa, 1897.

SCHREIBER, Darren, 'Political Cognition as Social Cognition: Are We All Political Sophisticates?', Abstract submitted to The Political Dynamics of Thinking and Feeling, October 18, 2004.

SEEL, Martin – Art as Appearance: Two Comments on Arthur C. Danto's after the End of Art. History and Theory. Vol. 37, n° 4 (1998), pp. 102-114.

SEGRÉ, Monique, *L'École des Beaux-Arts: XIXe-XXe siècles*, Paris, Editions L'Harmattan, 1998.

SERRÃO, Vítor, *A Pintura Maneirista em Portugal,* Lisboa, Ministério da Educação, 1992.

Idem, *O maneirismo e o estatuto social dos pintores portugueses,* Lisboa, Imprensa nacional – Casa da Moeda, 1983.

Idem, 'O Pintor Régio Fernão Gomes, O Mosteiro da Anunciada e a Fundação da Irmandade de São Lucas, Corporação dos Pintores de Lisboa, em 1602', in GOMES, Ana Cristina, MOURÃO, José Augusto, FRANCO, José Eduardo & SERRÃO, Vítor (Coord.), *Monjas Dominicanas. Presença, Arte e Património em Lisboa,* Lisboa, Alétheia Editores, 2008, p. 112-121.

SERRÃO, Vítor, A Pintura Maneirista em Portugal, Lisboa, Instituto de Cultura e Lingua Portuguesa, 1991.

SHANKEN, Edward A., 'Art in the Information Age: Technology and Conceptual Art', in Leonardo, Volume 35, Number 4, 2002, pp. 433-438.

SHAW, Joyce Sutler – "The Anatomy Lesson": The Body, Technology and Empathy. Leonardo, Bol. 27, n° 1 (1994), pp. 29-38.

SILVA, Jorge Henrique Pais da, Páginas de História da Arte, Lisboa, Estampa, 1986.

SILVA, Jorge Henrique Pais da & CALADO, Margarida, Dicionário de termos de arte e arquitectura, Barcarena, Editorial Presença, 2005.

SILVA, Raquel Henriques da, Aurélia de Souza, Lisboa, Inapa, 1992.

SILVEIRA, Miguel de & SEMKE, Hein, *Exposição de escultura e cerâmica de Hein Semke,* Lisboa, Secretariado Nacional de Informação, 1947.

SIMÕES, Santos, Azulejaria em Portugal nos séculos XV e XVI: introdução geral, Lisboa, Fundação Calouste Gulbenkian, 1990.

SIMPSON, Miles – The Sociology of Cognitive Development. Annual Review of Sociology. Vol. 6, n° 1 (1980), pp. 287-313.

SMITH, Robert, The art of Portugal, 1500-1800, London, Weindenfeld and Nicolson, 1968.

SOARES, Ernesto, História da gravura artística em Portugal: os artistas e as suas obras, Lisboa, Samcarlos, 1971.

SOBRAL, Luís de Moura, *Pintura e Poesia na época barroca,* Lisboa, Editorial Estampa, 1994.

SOUSA, Frei Luís de & MURPHY, James Cavanah, Plans, elevations sections and views of the church of Batalha, in the province of Estremadura in Portugal, with the history and descruption by Fr. Luís de Sousa, London, Library of Fine Arts, 1836.

SOUSA, Pedro Manuel – Os exames de área na pintura de cavalete e o ensino experimental da Física. Faculdade de Ciências da Universidade de Lisboa, 2001, p. 11. Dissertação de Mestrado em Física para o Ensino.

SPIEGEL, Gabrielle M., 'Revising the Past / Revisiting the Present: How Change Happens in Historiography', in History and Theory, Volume 46, Number 4, 2007, pp. 1-19.

SPONSLER, Claire – Cyberpunk and the Dilemmas of Postmodern Narrative: The Example of William Gibson. Contemporary Literature. Vol. 33, No. 4 (1992), pp. 625-644.

STRATZ, C.H. – **La figura humana en el arte**. Barcelona: Salvat, 1926.

STUART, Barbara – **Analytical Techniques in Materials Conservation**. Chichester: John Wiley & Sons Ltd., 2007.

SYNNOTT, Anthony, 'Truth and Goodness, Mirrors and Masks – Part I: A Sociology of Beauty and the Face', in The British Journal of Sociology, Volume 40, Number 4, 1989, pp. 607-636.

SYNNOTT, Anthony, 'Truth and Goodness, Mirrors and Masks Part II: A Sociology of Beauty and the Face', in The British Journal of Sociology, Volume 41, Number 1, 1990, pp. 55-76.

T

TABORDA, José da Cunha – **Regras da arte da pintura: com breves reflexões críticas sobre os caracteres distintivos de suas escolas, vidas e quadros de seus mais célebres professores**. Coimbra: Imprensa da Universidade, 1922. Tradução da obra de Michelangelo Prunetti, *Saggio Pictorico*, publicado originalmente em 1786.

TETLOW, John – The Vocabulary of High-School Latin and How to Master It. The Classical Journal. Vol. 5, n° 1 (1909), pp. 18-29.

THOMPSON, Herb – Cybersystemic Learning. Radical Pedagogy (2001). Available

athttp://www.radicalpedagogy.org/radicalpedagogy/Cybersys
temic_Learning.html [17-05-2015].

THOMPSON, Timothy A. – Pórtico partido para o Impossível: Fernando Pessoa and the Portuguese Sublime. Portugueses Studies. Vol. 25, n° 2 (2009), pp. 151-168.

TOBIN, Richard, 'The Canon of Polykleitos', in American Journal of Archaeology, Volume 79, Number 4, 1975, pp. 307-321.

TOLEDO-PEREYRA, Luis H. – X-Ray Surgical Revolution. Journal of Investigative Surgery. Vol. 22, Issue 5 (2009), pp. 327-332

TOLEDO-PEREYRA, Luis H., 'X-Ray Surgical Revolution', in Journal of Investigative Surgery, Volume 22, Issue 5, pp. 327-332.

TOMASULA, Steve – Genetic Art and the Aesthetics of Biology. Leonardo. Vol. 35, No. 2 (2002), pp. 137-144.

TRINDADE, António, Um Olhar Sobre a Perspectiva Linear Em Portugal, Nas Pinturas De Cavalete, Tectos e Abóbadas: 1470-1816, Tese de doutoramento em Belas Artes, especialidade em Geometria Descritiva, Faculdade de Belas-Artes da Universidade de Lisboa, Lisboa, 2008.

Idem, 'Quatro baixos relevos italianos no mosteiro de Santa Maria Belém', in Revista Artis, Número 1, 2002, separata.

Idem, 'Geometria, perspectiva linear e escala teológica, pintura e contemporaneidade. Que futuro?', in Revista :Estúdio, Volume 5, Número 10, 2014, pp. 50-60.

Idem, 'A perspectiva linear na pintura: a família do Visconde de Santarém, de Domingos António Sequeira', in Arte Teoria, Número 12/13, 2010, pp. 133-138.

Idem, 'A recepção do modelo de perspectiva linear renascentista a norte e a oeste dos Alpes e um exemplo concreto no Museu Nacional de Arte Antiga em Lisboa', in Arte Teoria, Número 6, 2005, pp. 51-73.

TUSA, Erzsébet, 'Art Education, or the Art of Education', in Studia Musicologica Academiae Scientiarum Hungaricae, Volume 25, Issues 1-4, 1983, pp. 101-109.

U
URRY, John, The Tourist Gaze, London, Sage, 2001.

V

VARNHAGEN, Adolfo de, Noticia historica e descriptiva do Mosteiro de Belem, Lisboa, Typ. Da Sociedade Propagandora dos Conhecimentos Úteis, 1842.

VASARI, Giorgio, *Le vite de' piú eccellenti pittori, scultori e architettori*, Novara, Istituto Geografico de Agostini, 1967.

VASCONCELOS, Inácio da Piedade, *Artefactos symmetriacos, e geometricos*, Lisboa, Joseph Antonio da Sylva, 1733.

VASCONCELOS, Joaquim, Da architectura manuelina, Coimbra, Imprensa da Universidade, 1885.

VELTMAN, Kim H., 'Literature on Perspective: A Select Bibliography (1971-1984)', in Marburger Jahrbuch für Kinstwissenschaft, Volume 21, 1986, pp. 185-207.

VENABLE, Bradford, 'The"Iconologia": Helping Art Students Understand Allegory', in *Art Education*, Volume 61, Number 3, 2008, pp. 15-21.

VIEIRA, José António Jacinto, *História contemporânea da segurança e saúde na fase de concepção arquitectónica*, Dissertação de Doutoramento, Universidade Portucalense Infante D. Henrique, 2007.

VILELA, José Stichini – Francisco de Holanda: vida, pensamento e obra. Lisboa: Instituto de Cultura e Língua Portuguesa, 1982.

VELLEMAN, J. David – A Rational Superego. The Philosophical Review. Vol. 108, n° 4 (1999), pp. 529-558.

VERGEER, Wim C. – Σκια and Σωμα the strategy of xontextualisation in Colossians 2:17. A Contribution to the quest for a legitimate contextual theology today. Neotestamentica. Vol. 28, n° 2 (1994), pp. 379-393.

VITERBO, Sousa, Noticia de alguns esculptores portuguezes ou que exerceram a sua arte em Portugal, Lisboa, Typ. Lallement, 1900.

Idem, Noticia de alguns pintores portuguezes e de outros que, sendo estrangeiros, exerceram a sua arte em Portugal, Lisboa, Academia Real das Sciencias 1902.

VITRÚVIO, *Tratado de Arquitectura*, Lisboa, Instituto Superior Técnico Press, 2006.

W

WADSWAORTH, Barry J. – **Piaget's theory of cognitive and affective development**. 4ª Edição. New York: Longman, 1989.

WANG, Orrin N.C. – Jant's Strange Light: Romanticism, Preiodicity, and the Catachresis of Genius. Diacritics. Vol. 30, n° 4 (2000), pp. 15-37.

WARBURG, Aby, Atlas Mnemosyne, Madrid, Akal D.L., 2010.

WARD, Frazer, 'The Haunted Museum: Institutional Critique and Publicity', in October, Volume 73, 1995, pp. 71-89.

WARD, Martha, 'Impressionist Installations and Private Exhibitions', in The Art Bulletin, Volume 73, Number 4, pp. 599-622.

WARDRIP-FRUIN, Noah – Hypermedia, Eternal Life, and the Impermanence Agent. Leonardo. Vol. 32, No. 5 (1999), pp. 353-358.

WATTENWYL, André von; ZOLLINGER, Heinrich – Color-Term Salience and Neurophysiology of Color Vision. American Anthropologist. Vol. 81, n.° 2 (1979), pp. 279-288.

WIENER, Norbert – Cybernetics. New York: John Wiley & Sons, Inc., 1948.

Idem – Cybernetics or Control and Communication in the Animal and the Machine. Cambridge: MIT Press, 1961.

WECHSLER, Judith, 'Illustrating Samuel Beckett: The Issue of the Supererogatory', in Art Journal, Volume 52, Number 4, 1993, pp. 33-40.

WERCKMEISTER, Otto Karl, 'Marx on Idealogy and Art', in New Literary History, Volume 4, Number 3, 1973, pp. 501-519.

WESSELL, Leonard P., 'Alexander Baumgarten's Contribution to the Development of Aesthetics', in The Journal of Aesthetics and Art Criticism, Volume 30, Number 3, 1972, pp. 333-342.

WICKS, Robert, 'Kant on Fine Art: Artistic Sublimity Shaped by Beauty', in The Journal of Aesthetics and Art Criticism, Volume 53, Number 2, 1995, pp. 189-193.

WIERZBUCKA, Anna, 'Human Emotions: Universal or Cultural-Specific?', in American Anthropologist, Volume 88, Number 3, 1986, pp. 584-594.

WILLIAMS, John, 'Meyer Schapiro in Silos: Pursuing an Iconography of Style', in The Art Bulletin, Volume 85, Number 3, 2003, pp. 442-468.

WILLIAMSON, Jack H., 'The Grid: History, Use, and Meaning', in Design Issues, Volume 3, Number 2, 1986, pp. 15-30.

WINCKELMANN, Johann Joachim, Histoire de l'art dans l'antiquité, Paris, Librarie Génerale Française, 2005.

WÖLFFLIN, Heinrich, Conceitos fundamentais da História da arte: o problema da evolução dos estilos na arte mais recente, São Paulo, Martins Fontes, 1984.

WOOD, Francis A. – The Origin of Color-Names. Modern Language Notes. Vol. 20, n.º 8 (1905), pp. 225-229.

WORRINGER, Wilhelm, Abstracción y naturaleza, México, Fondo de Cultura Económica, 1953.

WYNNE, Vincent W. – Abraham's Gift: A Psychoanalytical Christology. Journal of the American Academy of Religion. Vol. 73, n° 3 (2005), pp. 759-780.

Y

YOUNGS, Amy M. – The Fine Art of Creating Life. Leonardo. Vol. 33, No. 5 (2000), pp. 377-380.

YU, Timothy – Oriental Cities, Postmodern Futures: "Naked Lunch, Blade Runner", and "Neuromancer". MELUS. Vol. 33, No. 4 (2008), pp. 45-71.

Z

ZAN, João Carlos – Ramalho Ortigão e o Brasil. São Paulo: Faculdade de Filosofia, Letras e Ciências Humanas da Universidade de São Paulo, 2009. Tese de doutoramento em Letras, especialidade de Estudos Comparados de Literaturas de Língua Portuguesa.

ZIZEK, Slavoj – **Organs without bodies**, Available athttp://www.lacan.com/zizsalsagon.html [12-06-2015].

®MurphyAlmeida